The Energy of
PLAY

The Energy of
PLAY

EDITOR
Erica Glessing

Compiled and edited by Erica Glessing

Copyright 2016 by Happy Publishing and Erica Glessing

First Edition

ISBN 978-0-9896332-9-1

Cover design by Melinda Asztalos

Interior design by Roseanna White Designs

No part of this publication may be translated, reproduced or transmitted in any form without prior permission in writing from the publisher.

Publisher and editor are not liable for any typographical errors, content mistakes, inaccuracies, or omissions related to the information in this book. Each point of view and chapter belongs to the individual author who submitted it. Each author owns the rights to his or her chapter. All of the authors in this publication have granted permission for inclusion of their photo and content.

Foreword

Heather K. Nichols

How often do you play? And what have you decided that play is, that limits how much play you can actually have in your life? The energy of play is practically obsolete in the world of adults. We have decided that it is not valuable, not useful, not practical, and won't further all of the things we are all so 'needing' to accomplish every day.

What if there was a different possibility? And what if everything is the opposite of what it appears to be? Would you be willing to entertain the idea that play can expand your life and all that you are creating dynamically, and with ease?

Has there ever been a time in your life when you have been incredibly joyful, playful, and happy? If so, what did you create then? How much ease did you have? So often when we are being the space of joy and play, we are being an energy that is totally generative, creative, and expansive. Some call it 'flow'… that space when everything seems to show up as if by magic and with total ease.

How elusive does that space seem to you? Often we think that space of play, joy, and ease is something that just kind of

Foreword ~ Heather K. Nichols

'happens' from time to time, when we are lucky, when the stars are aligned, or when all the proper conditions are met. How fun is that?! What if you could choose play and joy *first*—as the generative and creative energies that set in motion the ease of creation in your world, with you, and on your behalf?

So, how do you choose play and joy? You choose it! You choose to be and to have those energies as your life. You don't have to know 'how' that is going to show up, or what you can do to add more joy and play. What you do have to do, is to be willing to be judged as crazy, too happy, weird—and to be willing for people to not take you 'seriously'. Play and joy are not part of the adult world in this reality. Are you willing for them to be yours, no matter what? Is it time?

What's the worst that can happen? You could fail! And what if there's just nothing wrong with that?! When kids are playing, failure is not even a consideration in their world. They make things up, they make-believe, they adjust, they try new things, they create—with abandon. Nothing is failure in their worlds! They see their play as a constant space of creation.

How much would the willingness to fail expand in your life and your world? And the willingness to be judged? The more I'm willing to fail, flail, be judged, get it wrong, mess up—the more joy and the more play I have in my universe.

Failure is a judgment. Play is a choice.

If you knew you could never fail, what would you choose? And how much fun could you have?

Heather

Table of Contents

Chapter 1..9
GET READY, GET STARTED, PLAY!
Pia Jansson

Chapter 2..23
PLAYING WITH YOURSELF
Chelsea Gibson

Chapter 3..37
HOW BEING PLAYFUL IN LIFE CREATES GREATER JOY AND FULFILLMENT
Ashley Stamatinos

Chapter 4..49
THE POWER OF PLAY TO HEAL
Carrie Seela

Chapter 5..59
PLAYMATES IN THE STRANGEST PLACES
Ashley McCaughey

Chapter 6..67
PLAYING WITH THE LIGHT
Dr. Lisa Cooney

Chapter 7..81
GETTING TO PLAYFUL
Erica Glessing

Chapter 8 89
WHAT DOES PLAY MEAN TO YOU?
Susan Shatzer

Chapter 9 99
UNSNUFFING YOUR PLAYFULNESS AND ASKING QUESTIONS
Janie Smith

Chapter 10 119
DON'T MAKE ME GROW UP!!
Lisa Miller

Chapter 11 129
PLAYING WITH EVERYTHING
Christel Crawford

CHAPTER

1

Get Ready, Get Started, Play!

Pia Jansson

The energy of play, just saying it gets my mouth watering and body excited! Enticing, fun and available at a moments notice! I'm game, are you? How yummy is play for you? Do you allow yourself to play? Daily? Weekly? Monthly? Is it important to you? Do you actively seek it out or are you holding yourself back from it? What does the energy of play look like to you? What is your favorite expression of the energy of play?

There are so many choices, from the softer energies, to laugh out loud vivid high energy moments. Play to me is about spontaneous inspired actions outside-of-the-box of structure. The energies of play, curiosity, fun and laughter are often intertwined and play is how I often access my inner wisdom and creativity. Having an animated cheerleading type of personality by nature and a day job that includes "Activity" in the title, movement tends to evoke the energy of play for me and I love playing with people that allow the energy to flow in

the speed it desires, often very fast. It can be physical activity as well as something like a fun brainstorming session or singing to a song that inspires into a spontaneous dance. Not everyone allows themselves to play and for people like me who LOVE to play it's been interesting to see how I have allowed that to affect me at times.

I love being silly and have no problem making a fool of myself. I am comfortable on stage or in front of a group. Playing in the school orchestra, dance performances and even trying on some theater as a kid certainly helped me be comfortable on stage, yet at that time I didn't know what the energies were all about and would get nervous. I used to initiate play and get the crowds going at parties when I was younger and probably had even more fun than those I entertained. As the energy of the communities I interacted with changed, so did I and how I expressed it. With friends or on my own I generate it daily as the need arises, I am a spontaneous personality and when I have people and beings around me that enjoy playfulness, even more fun gets created. In public, with strangers in groups, I tend to wait for an invitation or dare to initiate something. I've realized in recent years that it has more to do with me tapping into the energy of the group than shyness, and I'm exploring what actions I can take to change that right now.

So I wonder, how much of the energy of play is simply about claiming it, choosing and then taking action, as with anything else in life? Does it even matter if people can receive it or not? It takes courage to get people started at least when the context around you isn't play. Yet a simple action like laughing out loud or dancing in the street can inspire others to join in and whether people join in or not how much fun are you having? And how much of an invitation for play are you being in these moments?

I know for me when I see someone expressing a playful energy

The Energy of Play

like that I'll smile, at a minimum, and pay that energy forth to the people I meet next with that smile on my face.

I'm the kind of person that tends to play full-out when I'm engaged, and no judgment can stop me. I lose all concept of time, get in the zone, and enjoy myself fully. I find that the energy of play is often associated with a physical activity whether movement is included or not, the body is engaged. And while playing with someone else can enhance the fun possibilities of play there is something about allowing play into your life when you're on your own too! Being playful is like breathing to me, on the scale of importance. It is something I prioritize and create daily if even for a moment, and the expressions of it vary. It's often a spontaneous action that I jump into full-on and just laugh as I experience it's unfolding. These energies that range from soft play to full out laughing out loud type of playfulness.

So while my idea or choice of play and fun may be completely different than yours I would like to invite you into my world of play. Maybe it will inspire you to explore new areas in your life where you can bring play into your day to day life if so desired?

Animals and Kids

I love observing kids and animals as they often approach play without a point of view. They just be and express a need in the moment until their done. I have a dog, an adorable and entertaining "Havanese" boy named Rocco, who for almost six years has entertained me daily with his playful energy and expressions. He inspires me and is a teacher in so many ways. I love to observe his choices and how he approaches play and life in general. Just going for a walk with him or bringing him along in the car on a road trip has me access the energy of play. He is a master of energy manipulation, we connect energetically and most often interact without words. He continually shows me what it's like to have no point of view when playing, he plays

when he desires and not when he's not up for it. You could say that we share the same sense of humor as it's not uncommon to see us running around the house, me playfully chasing him engaged in the energy of play, or playing catch and throwing the ball. He gets me laughing so hard and in action. I'm so grateful for this sweet being who has me laughing out loud daily with his charming personality and access to play. With him I access my inner child full on!

My office is surrounded by trees, and every day I get to watch the squirrels play, birds resting on a branch before taking off and the trees playing with the elements of wind, sun, rain and the beings that interact with them. Nature represents a calm energy of play as I'm the observer yet get to access the entertainment of all the critters "for free". It's really calming yet entertaining for me to just be with for a minute here and there throughout the day as I engage in the activities of my day job. At times, after observing all the fun outside my office windows my playful energy needs a release and I'll select a song in my iTunes library that inspires me and take a dance break.

And then there's observing kids. The other day I went to an outdoor mall nearby that caters to kids and pets too. It has a structure where you can climb and explore, that is normally filled with kids to the max (I wish it would hold adults too as I would be playing there in a heartbeat!). It boasts several water areas where splashing is a given. I was watching a girl playing with a boat floating back and forth in shallow waters. She was completely engulfed in her world of play, in the zone, with her mother watching nearby. That evoked memories in me when I was a kid and how I would be outdoors rain or shine and just run around and play with the neighborhood kids. Accessing the world of wonder where there are no limitations and just going with the flow of the game. Boys and girls playing together with no separation. I played a lot with the boys as I loved being

active climbing trees for one and being in nature which I had a lot of where I grew up. There was a lot of space to create play with trees, meadows, forests and even horses nearby. My inner child is still very much alive and eager to play! Who would like to join me?

Via channels like YouTube and Facebook, I get access to peek into the fun worlds of people around the globe. Just watching all the playful silliness of animals and kids just being in the moment activates that energy for me. The energy of play is in our being after all with infinite expressions and choices.

Branding and Growth

Another way that the energy of play is activated in me is anything related to personal growth. The modalities that I have been drawn to have included exploration of the mind, body, spirit, heart, you name it. Often through various play activities that had me and my peers stretch beyond our comfort zones. I've had so much fun! And that is why I continue choosing it.

Communicating with people that are willing to play full-out without ego or significance is priceless! I appreciate these moments, whether they involve a brainstorming session, an expansive awareness conversation, or an inquiry. I have always been fascinated about space on all levels, having expansive conversations in any area of life and to live and go beyond the "box" of whatever "normal" is.

In recent years I was introduced to the game of asking expansive questions and tapping into the energy of your awareness, where it's not about answering the question which is so much fun! As I have introduced this concept to my friends and communities it's been amazing to see the change that has been created with this playful approach and energy present.

What questions can you ask to create more play in your life? What conversations would you like to have? What would bringing the energy of play while asking questions add to your life?

Right now I'm looking into branding through a different lens than before. Having been on a mission to express the essence of who I am in the world I find the branding piece super fun. It's one of the areas in my life where a fire energy gets activated in my being and the creative juices get going. I've played with branding before and recently found someone who brought some new perspectives to it all that are fun.

You don't have to own a business to create yourself as a brand, after all you and your life is your business, what does your brand communicate about you? Is what's on the inside seen and expressed on the outside? Is the person you are infused into the branding of your business?

Right now I'm in the inquiry of whether my blogs and written communications match who I am in person, with my voice, vibe and external presentation. While I have to tone down my language in business correspondence, I am looking at how I can bring more of the playful energy of me into it. One of the elements that currently has me engaged in play mode are the Gallup StrengthsFinder 2.0 themes. Inquiring how I can integrate my being, strengths and talents into my daily activities with Positivity being my #2 theme. Blending all the different teachings I've been engaged in over the years together into a mix that is true to who I am while asking questions and tuning into my awareness. I'm excited what I will be creating and when I'm excited the energy of play is present. It's so expansive to me to focus on people's strengths whether expressed in their personalities or energy, ideally with it all blending together in harmony.

The Energy of Play

What playful energies of yours do you, or would you like to bring forth into your brand? Does your bio express your playfulness? Do you express your playfulness in your writing? Does the energy of play come out when you meet people face to face? If not, what actions could you take to bring it forth? What would be fun and true for you? If you were to create a logo that represented you, what would it look like? What colors and fonts would you be drawn to?

Clothing

Another of my fire energy actives of play is expressed in the world of my personal essence colors. I have invested many years with an intuitive color and fashion expert. The journey I embarked on when I first received my color palette based on the essence of my being was profound. I've played with this since 2005 on and off while learning and eventually mastering what to look for and what works for me (and others). It's been a very empowering and playful journey to explore and express with my inner child while playing a form of dress up.

What had me started on this journey initially was the invitation of "what walking into a room without uttering a word and people getting the essence of you would create" through your colors, clothing choices and accessories. It's an expression of play that keeps on giving, changing and expanding. Daring to be different and dressing uniquely as me, investing in pieces that I will wear independent on what's in fashion and integrating the pieces of the current fashion trends that work for me. In the end creating a unique style that is my expression in the world.

Have you ever wondered what your clothing, color choices and how you put it all together communicates about you? Inspired by the seasons of nature, the essence and colors that we each

uniquely have (hair, skin, eyes), wearing styles and fabrics that feel yummy on our body and also flatter our body shape independent on size brings it all together. This world of color inspires and evokes play in me to the core of my being and whether my clothing inspires other to play I do know that my choices allow me to express spur of the moment activities in a variety of ways without constraints. I'm comfortable with what I wear no matter what size my body is which keeps my playful energy alive and I know what colors I can play with to evoke different emotions while I communicate the essence of me.

When I'm in this community of color essence it's like an explosion of color, each person expressing themselves in their unique way all inspired by mother Earth and its seasons. When I'm with my essence sisters & brothers the bouncy and whimsical energy of play & laughter is present within moments.

So I wonder, what playfulness could you add to your wardrobe? What would adding your self-expression, essence and invitation of play look like and create in your life? Does the idea of expressing the playfulness of you in your clothing sound like fun? What colors evoke the energy of play in you? How do they make you feel? What could you create in the world if you choose to wear colors and styles that bring out your essence of play? I wonder what that could add and create?

Design

Design engages many of my favorite play activities into one. I enjoy playing with different ideas whether I'm creating an outfit, a flyer or re-designing a room in my home. Tuning into the energy of the colors that inspire me, what combinations I can create with the energy that represents me and what I desire to feel or express in that moment of time. Allowing my playfulness shine through in my unique way that activates the

The Energy of Play

core of my being full on.

It never ceases to amaze me how a simple change like a different color on the wall, pillows, or simply rearranging the furniture in a room can create a big energy transformation both visually and emotionally. No matter what your budget is if you have $40, then paint alone goes a long way. Design and color go hand in hand, and evoke different energies for us all. Added to that are the styles we are drawn to, contemporary, modern, coastal, cozy are all part of my expression.

What styles do you enjoy? What makes you feel supported, happy, inspired and free to create your life? What would your expression look like if you allowed yourself to dream full out? What if you created a collage of images that represented the energies of how you would like to live your life? What if the energy of play as you choose to express it in the world would be infused in every area of your life? I wonder what yumminess you would create in the world from the space and energy of play?

Entertainment and Theme Parks

Have you ever been to a water park? Or places like Walt DisneyWorld®, Universal Studios or Six Flags®? Interactive places like Dave & Buster's? What I love about these types of places is that they are setup for play for all ages. When I'm in play mode I tend to go full out, totally engulfed in the moment and energies of play. It's one of the areas that I would like to play more in, would you like to join me? Then there are board games, whether it's Truth or Dare®, Monopoly®, or any game that occurs as fun in the moment, how much fun is that? Going on scavenger hunts, and participating in other fun group games?

What activates and energizes play for you in these areas? Is there

something calling you right now that would be fun to engage in? Would dusting of that game hidden away in storage that you couldn't part with be a contribution? Who can you invite to play with?

Physical Activities

So the most obvious activity that evokes the energy of play for me is anything physical. Whether I'm playing beach volleyball, rollerblading, bike riding, kickboxing, engaging in water activities or animated physical games, climbing trees, dancing or having sex the possibilities are infinite of what can be created. It's the "in the zone" type of activities that are so expansive and fun, and yes, laughter is often included.

Photography

I love taking pictures, being silly and doing whatever it takes to bring out the playfulness, joy and laughter in the people I photograph. It's another activity that activates my creative fire energy and access to play. Photography has me so energized, whether I'm behind the camera or in front of it, independent of the subject. Playing with people is extra fun though and I recently had my first professional photoshoot with two wonderful ladies that specialize in what I love to express myself, natural light photography.

While they specialize in bringing out the essence of each woman they photograph and they do, with breathtakingly beautiful photographs of each goddess, my focus is slightly different. My experience from my session in front of the camera was gold, before, during and after my session, I was ready and had so much fun. When I'm playing with people that can communicate the parts of me that are true for me, it expands on the playful energy I naturally am. The photographs while a snapshot of a moment in time, there is still a palpable

The Energy of Play

energy that can be tapped into long after. My bio image is one of them.

I play with men and women willing to let loose and engage in play and laugh at my silly energy and directions while I photograph them. *So I wonder, do you/are you willing to access and bring forth the playful energy of you in public? Does being in front of the camera excite you? Would it be fun and playful? What would your expression of play look like if you were in front of a camera? Who would you like to have take your pictures? What style of photography would bring out your energy of play? What is your unique expressions and gifts of play?*

So I leave you with these questions to ponder should you choose to.

What season(s) are you drawn to?
What happens in nature during that time?
Would using that as an inspiration or invitation open up something new for you?
Do you love to play and make it happen all year around?
Are you someone who secretly enjoys getting other people going or do you enjoy others inviting you into play?

Writing this chapter has been another way for me to tap into the energy of play and my takeaway is how much joy it is for me to write. It is my hope that I will have inspired you to engage in some new energy of play after reading this chapter and would love to hear what you got out of it. You can reach me at www.space-2-play.com.

Here are some of the resources that inspire me to play that are mentioned in this chapter:

Access Consciousness® - www.accessconsciousness.com
> "Access Consciousness offers you the tools and questions to create everything you desire in a different and easier way and to change the things in your life that you haven't been able to change until now. It empowers you to know that you know and provides you with ways to become totally aware and to begin to function as the conscious being you truly are."

Jennifer Butler Color - www.jenniferbutlercolor.com
> "Tap into the secret of your unique color palette. More than 90% of all communication is nonverbal. Your unique color palette empowers you, attracts others and creates focus. Your palette informs your wardrobe, interiors, personal and company branding. During your Personal Color DNA Profile master colorist Jennifer Butler will draw from more than 4,000 color swatches to find the unique color harmonies that give you the greatest psychological advantage."

In Her Image Photography - www.inherimagephoto.com
> "Step into your power. Honor your journey and embrace your authentic self. You are beautiful. You are magnificent. Remind yourself. Remind the world. This is your time to shine."

Amazing goddess photography that brings out the essence of each woman they photograph. These lovely ladies took the picture in my bio and several more on my website.

SmartyPants Branding - www.daniellemmiller.com
> "Personal brand specialist. Brand with bold soul + red hot strategy. Isn't it time for your brand to be the one others crush on?"

About the Author

Pia Jansson

As far back as I can remember I've been sought out for advice, personal and business, while I was exploring different paths for myself. I tend to have the ability to create a safe space for people to relax and be themselves. I love to inspire and be part of the process of facilitating change in people's lives in a playful, empowering, positive and casual way. Balancing flow and a focused kick in the butt get into action mode. Continual growth and exploration of who I am, shedding values and beliefs that no longer serve me to free up the space to be me, all of me, all the time, is a moment by moment choice that I prioritize in my life. I thrive on change and learning new things every day, being playful, silly, having FUN, and laughing daily. Having acted on impulses throughout my life I've created many learning lessons that in the end always have turned into gratitude. I am fascinated about space on all levels, having expansive conversations in any area of life and to live and go beyond the "box" of whatever "normal" is.

I am an Access Consciousness® Bars Practitioner and an ordained Minister through the Universal Life Church Monastery.

I've spent many years in the corporate world, building and re-organizing business areas and I also started up a subsidiary from scratch as as one of the co-creators instrumental to creating the foundation that exists today. My philosophy in general is that what I don't know I'll figure out.

Are you ready to explore what you would like to create? Play outside of the box with something new? Willing and ready get into action?

I will approach the areas of your needs from a multitude of directions, asking questions that may occur as random until it is all pulled together. I will find a positive angle and strategy to create and motivate from. I will look at what your strengths are and create something even better from there. I tend to be inspired by the future and what could be and put my thoughts into suggested actions. Are you ready to have fun and try a new approach? You can reach me at www.space-2-play.com.

2

Playing with Yourself

Chelsea Gibson

How often are you encouraged to play with yourself? I host a radio show called *Own Your Energy*, and I launched a show titled *Playing With Yourself*. I received some of the most interesting feedback about the title of the show. I had people from all over the world who were confused, turned on and curious.

It occurred to me the only time adults were told to play with themselves is when there is the connotation of masturbation. This was surprising to a person who has spent their life playing with herself. The energy of play for me is a way of living. It isn't a moment of time allocated to something fun and it is not only a way of sexually being with myself. The energy of play is a way of embodying that allows you to live without judgment and without the fear of mistakes. You are just playing right? Through personal stories and anecdotes, I will invite you to a new way of perceiving and being in the world through the energy of play.

Allow me to be an invitation for you to embody playfulness through the entirety of your life, your body and your spirit.

A Playful Girl in a Serious World

How I entered the world isn't surprising to most people who know me. While pregnant my mother thought something was wrong since I hadn't moved or kicked in days and so she went to the doctor. It turned out I just had no more room left. I had got so big I ran out of space. That was the beginning of what would be a common theme throughout my life. As I grow mentally, spiritually and physically I required more space.

While my mother was in labor the doctor and nurses stepped out of the room after hours of pushing without a budge. That was the moment I chose to start crowning. My father told my mom to push as he yelled out to doctors and nurses for assistance. As my head popped out he started realizing that he was going to be the one to catch me. Doctors came rushing in, cleaned me up and placed me in my father's arms. To this day he recalls touching my hands and saying to my mother "these are such special hands."

After my time confined in the womb you couldn't confine me in car seats or high chairs. I didn't desire to be wrapped in blankets and would lay down arms expanded. I required space. Even as a baby I was aware of my physical space and required lots of it. From my point of view as a child the world was a place of over stimulus. I was sensitive to food, emotions, texture, clothing, smells, sight and sound since a baby. This all seems so serious, however, my childhood never felt traumatic.

As a child energy and spirituality was my norm. It was neither a religious belief nor the influence from my family. I would put my hands of flowers and say I was helping them grow. My father was shocked at my hands healing capabilities. Without any prior knowledge of healing touch, he was sure I had a very special healing capacity. I was never taught to heal or to play with energy. It was second nature to use my hands and energy to heal and make people feel better. "I heal you, daddy" I would say.

Philosophy was a play place to explore my thoughts and ideas. My grandmother was an artist who would have me play with her professional paint. I remember as a young girl she said "There is never a mistake in art, you can always turn it into something else and it becomes part of the painting." This statement lasted throughout my childhood as a staple foundation to remind myself that mistakes in paintings were much like mistakes in life. Art was playful, as we were not trying to create Van Goh paintings. It was used for expression and space to play. Mistakes in art were just like mistakes in life and become part of your life. All you do is continue painting on and recreate something out of the mistake. It was a profound moment in my life.

The impact she had on my life was immeasurable through her patience with my stubbornness and sensitivities. She would tell my mother often to be patient with me and that my stubborn personality would one day be my biggest strength. She taught me how to play in the garden and how if you smell flowers when you are upset your whole world will calm down. My grandmother knew that my sensitivities were a gift that I had. Everyday simple experiences were an ever-evolving adventure for a child who is sensitive.

Dreaming was a time to soar to new places and float above my body. My mother has memories of me asking questions about spiritual topics such as floating away from my body when I slept at the age of five. I had an affinity for philosophy and asking questions about the children of the planet. I recall

speaking to angels and other entities as my confidants to ask questions about the unknown.

I was always playing. Not just with toys but with ideas, my body, my identity and the world around me. Nothing was off limit to play with. Both my parents worked in the airline industry and thus we travelled around the world exploring new cultures. I was privileged to have the world as my playground to create who I was and explore the vast ideas I was working out in my head. I would tell my younger brother tales of beings while pointing at clouds in the window of the airplane. When talking about the energy of play it seems as though people assume play requires being jovial. This was not true for a playful girl in a serious world. There seemed to be ideas, concepts and dimensions to play with even though they were deep in nature.

My body was the place that I did not have the same ease playing in. I loved exploring the philosophies in my head and distasted the sensations in my body. I was a goofy, silly and very deep girl when it came to just being with my thoughts. I told my grandmother my favorite thing to do was to spit and scream. She understood these were ways to release all the energy I had and was just part of the play. There was more difficulty with my body as I suffered from earaches and pains regularly. Walking for instance seemed difficult and uncomfortable. I would choose not walk on sand because I didn't like the texture for instance. Doctors found that my hips were misaligned on the right side and gave my parents special shoes for me to wear that would force my feet out and a brace at night to turn my hip inwards. After nights of terrifying screams and horrifying sleeps my mother chose to not continue the treatment. When playing in my body I was slow, patient and careful unlike the unconfined playfulness I had with my thoughts and imagination. Once I felt that my body was wrong after already being so sensitive within the confines of it I was never really comfortable in it again until my twenties. It was the first time I remember feeling the energy of judgment towards my body.

My grandmother who was the most patient person with my sensitivities and had special quotes for when I was upset died just before my sixth birthday. Not far after that I went through a series of testing for disabilities such as autism, Asperger's, and other learning disabilities. My sensitivities to the world concerned my mother. I had a difficult time learning routines in ballets classes and gymnastics for instance. My teacher once expressed it was as if I didn't know where my body was and what was left and what was right. I had a lack of body awareness although I had awareness of the micro level stimulus that surrounded me. My grandmother was a great teacher on how I could use my sensitivities as a gift and when she passed it was difficult to feel understood. At the end of the testing the doctor told my mother that my intelligence made it difficult for a diagnosis. Already at age six I had created schemas and short cuts in my mind that would allow me to problem solve different ideas and make a proper diagnosis difficult. It was the first time I felt the energy of judgment towards my intelligence.

I continued to be goofy and silly in play while expressing concerns for the poor and the hungry. One of my favorite games was to play homeless in the backyard. I knew that my life was privileged and that I took my life for granted. I was concerned at the amount of food waste and as such chose to pretend I was homeless to explore what it felt like. I transformed a deep concerning thought into something to play with. I naturally began meditating at eight years old when I would sit in quietude on a regular basis before bed. I recall this time being time to reconnect myself, ground and gather my thoughts. I've collected journal entries from this age which consisted of poems about going to my special place in my head where we could play all day in the sun, nature was everywhere

and my house was busy with four children and two working parents. This was my calm world.

At eight I was put into special programming to assist me in schoolwork and the diagnosis I was assigned was short-term memory disability. When the program began teaching me through playful skits and memory games the difficulties that I had in the classroom disappeared. It exchanged a serious focused style of learning to one of interest and intrigue.

By age 10, I began asking my mother whom mother earth had sex with to create the children of the planet based on my knowledge of my father and her having sex to create us. When she asked me what I thought I replied "with father sun" as I nodded and walked away pleased. I explored religion and churches during this time. I was fortunate to have a family that would accommodate taking me to different churches and allow me to explore. I would pray daily and would have conversations with an entity which I called father sun. During this time, we looked at a house on the outskirts of Calgary to possibly move to. As I walked through the house I began to express my memories of living in that very house. I described to my father the stairs, the closet to the left with a secret passage door. As we explored the house the description I gave was precise. We had never been to that house before. My intuition and awareness was increasing, and with the help of an open minded family I was able to explore these gifts and abilities.

When asked what I wanted to be when I grew up I said a dream psychologist. I began cataloging my dreams and learning to lucid dream. I would use the things in school and in books to change and play in my dreams. I started to read books on dream theory. As a young girl my favorite movies was the English Patient although I played with Barbie's until twelve. There was a recurring theme of being an extremely playful girl

while living in a world that was very serious with deep meaning.

I began to play with my identity, clothing, music preferences and friend groups through Junior high school and high school. I explored blonde hair and cheerleading to rainbow hair and punk music while continuing to play with video editing and photography. Videography and photography replaced my poetry as a way of expressing myself. I would play with equipment, camera tricks and editing without any advanced equipment and with zero training. My grandmother's lesson on mistakes in art transformed my ability to do art and express myself without judgment. Throughout the entirety of my self-exploration I kept a solid foundation of who I was. During the years of punk music and rainbow hair I continued to be an honor roll student, holding a volunteer position at a daycare, I was a yearbook editor and two jobs so I could pay for my sponsor child. As I explored different avenues of being I refused to buy into the entirety of the clothing style, music scene or friend group. Life was about exploring myself. There wasn't enough space to confine or describe me within dogmas and stereotypes. Play was integrating throughout the entirety of my adolescence as a way of exploring myself and different ways of looking, acting, being and expressing. The greatest friends I had through these years were the friends in allowance of my sensitivities and who wanted to play too.

With this brief description of my childhood you may start to understand the reasons why I have been able to play within the serious throughout my life. I have always been sensitive to energy, emotions and stimulus. This created a mental environment that was deep and serious although it isn't always understood. The people in my life with the most positive impact were those who were patient and gentle with me. I have managed to continue to embody the energy of play in my career, academics and personal healing journey based not only

on my nature but also from my Grandmother's point of view that you can never make a real mistake. As a therapist and professional healer I now can invite others to the energy of play through sessions and workshops. My sensitivities, playfulness and seriousness are all some of my greatest gifts. How can we integrate playfulness as adults? How can we be playful during work, in our relationships and in our theoretical views of life? All you have to do is start playing.

Playing with Your Energy

After a childhood of knowing and using energy it never occurred to me that we weren't made up of molecules that we can transform and play with. First it is important to recognize that you have a unique energy. Did you know that people could feel your energy when you walk into a room? Through meditation and different healing modalities from around the world I have learnt to transform my energy and move it. Different masters and shamans would call me a natural. Some were impressed with my ability to play with the modality and were curious at how I explored and integrated the different modalities and beliefs.

I was sitting in a intense meditation ceremony looking around the room and perceiving the struggle and drama others were having. As I sat there I looked down at my hands and could perceive my energy and I started to play. I wiggled my fingers and started creating energy balls. I could use energy to move my body and then started using my breath to direct my energy. It was all play!

Where have you decided that anything spiritual, emotional or even physical had to be serious? I like to subtly play with energy all day including with my water, food, space and my body. I play all day; I've had people ask me how often I do clearings or

energy practices. I reply "all day!" I do it all day. It isn't something I do as a regime or moment of time in meditation. It is a way of being.

I took my first class in Access Consciousness in June of 2014. I showed up in Amsterdam from Canada without any prior knowledge of what the class was or who Gary Douglas (the founder) was. It just felt like something I wanted to do and so I followed my gut instinct. Access Consciousness is a set of tools and processes that provides you with ways to become aware and ways to become the conscious being that you actually are. I had an Access Consciousness facilitator months after say to me that I "inspire her to play with the tools of Access Consciousness." We were sitting waiting for our sushi to arrive. I began to use the Access tools in a playful tone and doing the clearings that I had learned so that our sushi could come quicker. She had spent a long time with the tools but somehow made them more work and less playful. Are you taking the tools of Access, meditation, spirituality, fitness, and nutrition work? How fun is that? Did you know there is a way to honor the tools while approaching them in a playful way? From my point of view there isn't a lot of form and structure, everything is malleable and able to be played with. Would you be willing to play and when it stops working play with something else? Every time I learn something new I integrate it into my repertoire rather than becoming the tool or becoming the dogma. I continue to be myself and play with myself regardless of where I am or what I am learning.

What if your life was a playground? What is the path to enlightenment was paved with play? I have noticed that when I take the approach of play when approaching anything I take the judgment out of it. I give myself permission to learn and be the nurturing energy for myself to grow. I go back to the energy of what my grandmother taught me that day finger painting. If we

are playing with our lives, we can make mistakes and move on with ease. When taking the approach to play with your energy you don't require a dogma or belief to hold onto. All you do is learn a new way of perceiving you and the universe. You learn tools to integrate and transform your energy.

What if you are what you've been looking for?

If you watch children play there is a sense of freedom. There is freedom to laugh, fall, explore and make believe without judgment. This is the energy that you will receive when you begin to play with yourself. You can play with your energy, your body and your life. You owning your energy and playing with your energy is about creating and exploring. Then when something isn't working or a perceived mistake is made you can do something different or make a different choice. Since getting out of judgment of me, I have a sense of ease with my body, mental states, happiness and life purpose. Shopping, learning something new, travelling, fitness and work is done in a playful way. That is when I know I am being myself rather than how I am supposed to be.

I know deep down in myself I create everything in my life and thus I can uncreate it and recreate something else. What if all the things in life could be played with including yourself? You can create yourself and your identity through exploring new ways of being, thinking and perceiving the world. We haven't been taught to embrace the energy of play as adults unless it is a specified moment of fun or a moment of masturbation. Know that playing with yourself can be a moment of fun; a time of masturbation and also the way you approach life.

Embodiment of the Energy of Play

To embody the energy of play you've got to be the energy of play. This means it isn't about a particular activity or a moment allocated to something fun. I embody play by being the energy of it in every moment. The energy of play is life. It is the matter and source we create and explore life from. It is the ability to create, think and be with no judgments of you. In the energy of play mistakes seize to exist because it is part of the nature of play. Here lies the joy and ease of life. There is no pressure to win Nobel prizes, work for a multibillion-dollar company, look a certain way or have a perfect family. Embodying the energy of play is to embody the energy exploration. There is not an end goal in which you judge yourself by in this way of being because you're just playing. You can have targets that you play with instead and maybe you end up winning a prize, becoming rich or marrying your dream person. You could also create something better than you imagined or what you ever thought possible.

If life is a playground in which you are meant to learn, explore, grow and experience than you will find yourself making attempts, making believe and creating your life. You may actually have fun as well. As you recall from my childhood story that to play does not mean to not be serious or disrespect your life. On the contrary it is to play with the seriousness of life.

Did you know failing is part of learning? More so did you know if you fail or make a mistake that doesn't mean you're a bad person? What if you could explore life and not have to be perfect at everything all the time? What if life isn't a competition but rather a playground? How could this mindset change your life and relationship to yourself? You could start to explore the world and know that you are learning and playing. You have got to get that you are a very tall child who is just growing. You are always growing! The only constant in the universe is change itself! Do flowers ever go "I'm good as a bud and now I will be like this forever"? No! They blossom or they die.

Playing with Yourself ~ Chelsea Gibson

Are you dying inside? How many people on the planet are dyeing inside because they aren't allowing themselves to grow, change and play? Let's start to unlock mistakes as growth opportunities! While being on the planet know you will fall, say silly things and look funny. When did you buy that once you were an adult you had to know everything and be good at everything? It is time to create something that has never existed on planet earth and it begins with you. This is what I see people struggle with all areas of their life. They believe that if they take things serious enough they will succeed and then they allocate time to play through escapism. These types of people have chosen that life is serious and the only ways to get a break is to escape. Life is serious and full of judgment but you don't need to be part of it. If you could play all day would you have the need to escape? It is time to create something that has never existed on planet earth and it begins with you.

I will tell you now that there is more to life than a life of judgment and heaviness. Life can be the energy of play all the time. You have the ability to play and explore who you are and who you would like to be. Did you know you have the power to participate in creating a world you would like to live in? You can use the energy of play to create a body you would like to live in and an energy you would like to be. When you are present with that energy you will be the change the world requires. I realize now that me not being myself and not creating my life is the biggest disfavor I can do for the world. It is the same for you too! You embracing, exploring, playing with and being the energy that is you is the biggest contribution you can be to you and the planet. Try playing with yourself, life be more fun than you ever imagined!

About the Author

Chelsea Gibson

Chelsea Gibson is the CEO of Wild Rose Wellness and is a Cognitive Behavior Therapist, Access Bars Facilitator and Energetic Facilitator. Through her own evolution mentally and spiritually Chelsea realized her childhood passion for energy, meditation and helping people was reignited through her Business.

Chelsea has continued to travel around the world learning different tools in Access Consciousness, meditation, spiritual traditions, workshops and tools for a happier and healthier life to be able to provide a wide variety of services and perspectives for her clients. She now provides private sessions as well as teaches workshops and certifications in a variety of modalities and topics in the hopes of facilitating people on being more playful with creating their lives and bodies. Chelsea has an energy that is addictive to be around. Just try to not smile and laugh with this potent and bubbly being! Don't be fooled, when push comes to shove Chelsea will be able to blast your limitations and expectations away. She is gifted with helping people get to know their own bodies, and get into joyful communion with them. You can find her at www.WildRoseWellness.net.

CHAPTER

3

How Being Playful in Life Creates Greater Joy and Fulfillment

Ashley Stamatinos

It wasn't until I was in college that I realized I had been missing out on one of the greatest joys in life. I grew up rather serious and very focused. Even though I had plenty of fun as a young child and I was silly, of course, it was not until I stepped into my freshman year in college and met my new roommates, that I started to lighten up and see that I wasn't really being playful in life at all.

I wouldn't have actually labeled myself as uptight or too serious, but I certainly didn't (yet) possess the playfulness that my new friends easily embodied. I watched my friends as they laughed about the most serious of things and easily brushed off difficulties and obstacles.

I, on the other hand, made everything in my life important and took any obstacles I encountered to heart. I didn't even realize that the way I was functioning not only was not fun, but it was also sucking the joy out of my life.

I now lovingly look back at those first years in college with my lifelong friends and see it as a form of boot camp that they offered me.

They taught me to lighten up and not take everything so seriously. They taught me to get out of defense mode and to laugh more. They introduced me to silly movies and they specialized in inappropriate jokes.

I remember frequently dancing when there was no music playing and together we had no fear of being joyful and almost making fools of ourselves anywhere we went.

These friends taught me how to find humor in just about anything. They had a light-heartedness about them that was contagious, and I too started to see how I could create my life with a playfulness that I didn't know existed.

Having a Playful Outlook Enriches Your Life

Being playful and lighthearted is seemingly very un-natural for some of us. If you didn't grow up surrounded by people who could teach you to laugh frequently and not take yourself or your life too seriously, you probably don't function from that space.

In order to have a playful outlook on life, we need to teach ourselves to do this and consistently choose to live this way. I remember back in college when I first started to break free of my serious self, I was using the fake-it-til-you-make-it motto. This worked really well for me to get started.

I think the biggest key to living in joy, is to stop taking yourself so seriously and stop making everything in your life so significant. When you let go of the heaviness of everything in your life by making the choice to do so, you free yourself.

In essence, being serious and not engaging in play within your life is blinding you from seeing how you can enrich your existence and brighten your every day.

When you wake up in the morning you can ask the question, "I wonder how joyful and playful I can be today?"

When I ask this question before my feet hit the floor in the morning, I'm
setting up my day in a way where I'm looking for joy and I feel myself immediately being lighthearted and playful with myself and those around me.

You can choose how you'd like your day to unfold. You can create your life as you'd like it to unfold instead of just going along with the way things happen to show up for you.

We All Define Play Differently

Throughout this book, you'll read many different suggestions and definitions on what the energy of play and being playful means to the authors. I'd like to offer you the perspective that we all have unique view points and ways of looking at how we can best utilize the energy of play within our lives to create a life that is better than how we were previously living.

When you read all of the different suggestions given to you throughout this book, look for the stories, tools and teachings that resonate most with you and start there.

You don't need to implement every single tip or every suggestion. Simply listen to your gut and stick with what makes your feel lighter and happier just by reading it.

I'd like you to ask yourself this, "If I was truly being playful in my life, what would that look like for me?" Now, pause for a moment and see what pops into your mind before you keep reading.

(I want you to get an awareness of what being playful means to you before I tell you what it means to me.)

Now that I'm successfully a long time alum from what I affectionately call the "boot camp" that my friends gave me, I have a flood of images that enter my mind when I think of what being playful actually means to me. I immediately think of smiling and laughing along with images of feeling the wind in my face.

I think about working with clients that are serious and laughing with them to lighten the mood and help them see that they can choose to lighten their situation by shifting their mindset or energy.

Being playful to me is asking the universe (or God) questions, and knowing that I'll always get an awareness as a response. That feels playful to me because I feel like I have tools that give me the confidence to believe that no matter what obstacle or challenge I'm facing, I know I can change it.

My son has given me a fresh perspective on being playful in life and I have let go of limiting points of view that I didn't even know I had. Every time I let go of what's limiting me in my mind or in my life, I feel lighter and freer to play.

Being playful in life is when you're able to invite someone to step out of their comfort zone and see that they are more capable then they previously realized.

Whatever being playful means to you, I assure you that your definition will change and shift the more you lean into it. It will grow and expand and shift with you as you grow, expand and shift within your life.

Keep asking yourself on a regular basis, "Where in my life could I be more light-hearted and playful, and how much more joy could that welcome into my life?" See what opens up for you if you keep asking that question.

The Vulnerability of Living Life Playfully

Most people on earth thrive by holding onto their points of view and their judgments. Not as many people gauge their life's fulfillment based on how much they are able to enjoy every moment of their lives.

I have a coaching practice where I help people remove their limitations so they can step into a life they love. One of the biggest surprises I had within the first few years of my practice was that most people are not even looking for happiness, and to many people, having a playful outlook on life was more of an offense to juggle rather than a desirable goal.

It's scary to be judged as different or weird. It requires a certain level of vulnerability to allow yourself to open up, push down the barriers, remove the blinders and increase your ability to have fun with life.

Most people think it's scarier to be happy and joyful than sad and depressed. It takes a great strength to be vulnerable and show your true self. When you're willing to be in that place of vulnerability, that's where you can truly let go and lean into being playful to create more space for joy.

The most authentic beauty in life comes when you're willing to be yourself, without apologizing. You are honoring the deepest parts of you when you allow yourself to lean into life with a sense of gratitude, wonder and play.

What Does Living Playfully Look Like?

I've realized from the many people I've spoken with about this topic that we all have very different definitions of what we consider fun or what brings us joy. Equally so, we all have different definitions and different levels of intensity when explaining what it looks like to be playful within your life.

For me, I've found that the more I lean into being playful, the deeper my joy grows and that leads me to a greater sense of fulfillment.

Over the years, I have shifted and changed the way I am playful with life. My playfulness deepens all the time. I find when I ask the universe questions, magic shows up and I suddenly feel like I have a tool to change anything! This makes me smile and brings me to a childlike place where I can see the magic all around us and within us.

For instance, I would say I am playful within my business. I wake up in the morning and I ask my business questions to start the day. I ask, "Business, what do you require of me today? and "What can I create today that would be fun for me?"

After I ask the questions, I simply let it go. I don't look for an immediate answer; I just know that the universe will provide

magical responses for me at some point.

Being playful with life also means to have a light heart about things. I have worked hard to not take things personally. When someone judges you, it's always about them... not you. This was a key element that gave me the courage to be vulnerable and light-hearted about almost everything in life.

When I say I'm light-hearted about almost everything in life I mean that. For instance, when a client calls me, I have found that we create much greater results by working through traumas with laughter instead of crying.

People often comment on how I can make any heavy situation light. To me, that's the willingness to not buy into other people's point of view that life needs to be heavy. If I buy into their reality of what's going on for them as real and heavy than I'm helping them ground in that belief, giving it roots that will grow.

When I'm working with someone who is telling me about one terrible experience after another, I'll listen and interject a giggle while still sensitive to their situation; it will totally break up the negative energy. We always have a choice about how we look at things. Sometimes not buying into the heaviness around you is the greatest gift to the people around you and yourself.

Childlike Playfulness

I'm a mom to a super aware child. I knew before he was born that I needed to recognize that he was here to teach me a lot! Most times while raising your child, you focus on all the things you need to teach your child and we forget about all the beautiful gifts your child is ready to share with you.

There was no exception here. My son has always had endless

energy and he finds the smallest things funny. His playfulness with everything inspires me to bring more laughter and light-heartedness into all of the areas of my life.

He reminds me that as adults we don't' need to be so serious all the time. We can choose to laugh more and find the humor in seemingly mundane tasks.

As we grow older we gain more responsibilities and inevitably we get stressed more often. We can continue to move along this path as the majority of others do around us, or we can choose to see the magic in every moment.

This is again where vulnerability comes into play, because in order to be different/playful/joyful, we have to be willing to be vulnerable. Most people feel that the older you get, the more serious you must be. What if that were not true for you? What if the older you got the more in touch you became with your childlike self? Would that be fun for you?

What if you splashed in puddles when no one was looking, or you allowed yourself to fill up with excitement about a gift?

You have the capacity to see life through a new lens. You can choose to go through life and see the good in everything and look for what makes you smile… then ask for more of that.

If you are willing to be different and don't care if anyone judged you for it, who would you be and how would you act? Would you laugh more? Would you be freed up to see the small pleasures in life that were always there, but were hiding in plain sight because you were concerned about how you'd be judged?

The Energy of Play

Having Fun is Good for Your Health

When we stop having fun in our lives, we start creating greater stress, sometimes even depression and those can (and usually do) lead to health consequences. Stress is the number one cause of health problems.

When we choose to be light hearted and playful instead of going into the heaver emotions like stress or sadness, your body will thank you and ask for more playfulness.

I recently understood something that I had been hearing for years, but had not yet understood this message. Stress is a choice; being overwhelmed is a choice. So if these are all just choices, then it empowers you to choose something else if the experience of stress and being overwhelmed are not working for you.

When I finally started to understand this, I implemented it. I was looking at my to-do list that was a mile long and wanted to go into being both stressed and overwhelmed. Then I remembered that it's just a choice and I didn't have to choose to go into stress.

I felt so empowered to realize that I had this choice and truly didn't choose stress. Instead I chose to look at the humor of how long my list was and I chose to be lighthearted and playful about it. Instead of making it a doomsday scenario, I chose to laugh about it and take it piece by piece and find the joy in what I was working on. If I had succumbed to the stress of it all, I don't think I could have enjoyed the work that I was doing as I crossed things off my list.

I believe that when you allow yourself to be vulnerable, lighthearted and truly be yourself without apologizing, that's where you can access the depths of being playful and welcoming in more joy and fulfillment into every area of your world.

Life is a series of choices, and we have endless opportunities to keep choosing how we would like to create our lives every day. If you were to choose to live more playfully, would it allow you to have greater joy in your life? If you had greater joy in your life would you feel more fulfilled?

About the Author

Ashley Stamatinos

Ashley is the co-author of numerous #1 bestselling books, including The Energy of Expansion, and the Energy of Healing. She is widely known as the Empath Expert for her extensive work with highly sensitive people and she is an international speaker.

She has been interviewed on TV multiple times for her work with highly sensitive individuals. Her mission is to give you the tools to find inner peace within your busy life.

Ashley is the founder of Omorfi Healing, a business that she created as a platform to offer holistic education and healing to the world. She is passionate about teaching, and has been teaching for the last 10+ years. Within her practice she offers private coaching and both online and in-person courses to those seeking a life they love.

Wondering if you're an Empath? Take the free Am I an Empath?

Quiz on the home page of Ashley's website. (OmorfiHealing.com)

If you feel drawn to working further with Ashley on a one-on-one basis, you can go to her website and apply for a Free 30 Minute Clarity Call. (OmorfiHealing.com)

Ashley travels to guest lecture and teach her specialty classes. If you'd like her to come to your business to teach a course or to give a guest lecture, please email info@omorfihealing.com for further information.

Get Social with Ashley:

>Facebook.com/OmorfiHealing
>Twitter.com/OmorfiHealing
>YouTube.com/OmorfiHealing
>Pinterest.com/OmorfiHealing
>Periscope.tv/OmorfiHealing
>www.OmorfiHealing.com

CHAPTER

4

The Power of Play to Heal

Carrie Seela

When I think about the power of play, I think about splashing in puddles in the rain, about children playing in the park, laughter in the air, blowing bubbles and popping them before they float away, drawing on the sidewalk, dipping flowers in paint and placing them on paper, transforming nature into another form of art. These adventures have become part of my life while I have been a part-time nanny for my cousin's family. Chris (8), Cooper (5) and Emma (3) have been my playmates over the past several years. I have always enjoyed the pure and joyful energy children have. They are an example to me of living from the space of fun, joy, adventure, and laughter.

Being a nanny seemed like a great chance to reconnect with my own playful energy, after leaving a corporate job of 20 years. A big part of that decision was about having more fun and joy in my life. What better way to invite even more play into my adult life than spending time with children. They are ready to

try anything and I adore that enthusiasm. I had a playful side, but had spent years stifling that energy to be taken seriously at work. I was happy to be offered a job as a nanny and be paid to play. Chris, Cooper and Emma sparked my imagination and I discovered I liked to play just as much as they did.

I needed them more than ever when my world fell apart in April, 2012. My life changed in an instant when my mom had a brain aneurysm. She passed away a month later, never regaining consciousness. I watched life around me continue on as though nothing had happened, when my life and my heart had been shattered. I lost my brother five years earlier, so one would think that experience might have helped me in some way and maybe it did in ways I was not even aware of. Losing my mom was overwhelming. I did not realize how deep my relationship was with her on so many levels until she wasn't there. There were days when I wondered if the tears would ever stop. I had counted on her to be there for me. I wondered if I could go on without her.

Mom had always been my anchor. It was fun for me to go on new adventures with her encouraging me and cheering me on from a distance. I knew she would be there when I got home and I believe that allowed me to step out in a bigger way. We were more than mother and daughter, we were also the best of friends. People often commented about how close we were. We had always been close. The loss of my brother propelled me to leave my corporate job and launch myself into the world searching for something more. Her death made me want to shrink from the world and to withdraw into myself. I was completely lost. My stepdad, Don, was just as lost as I was and we looked to each other for comfort. I have always believed in the power of choice, but I had never been tested the way I was when Mom died. Part of me wanted to shrink from life and get small and invisible, only doing the bare minimum to survive,

The Energy of Play

but that would not be living. I had not left a job of 20 years only to sit on the sidelines and watch life pass me by.

Mom would not have wanted me to hide from the world. Her own spirit was bigger than life. She would have encouraged me to follow my heart and dare to be different. She would have encouraged me to have new adventures. I wanted that for myself as well. I knew I was not ready to give up on creating a fantastic life for myself and I also knew I would need some help and did not yet know what that might be or where it might come from.

In many ways, I felt like a child learning to walk as I learned to live without Mom. I felt uncertain and unbalanced, looking for support. I knew she was still there encouraging me from a different space. I heard the words she had spoken to me many times before, I am so proud of you, keep going. I was lucky enough to be surrounded by the joyful energy of Chris, Cooper and Emma.

Emma was only seven months old when Mom died and still required cuddling and holding. I transferred the love I had for Mom to the children. I didn't know what else to do with it. Emma even reminded me of Mom from her features to her spirit. Emma had big dark brown eyes and dark brown hair. She was a happy baby. She was quick to smile and laugh. It required my full attention to change diapers, get them dressed, fix bottles for Emma and peanut butter and jelly sandwiches for the boys. I read to them at night and put them to sleep. I didn't have time to dwell on my own loss when I was with them. They gave me space to have my tears when I felt sad. They would get quiet for a few minutes and sit with me only to pull me out of it ready to play and asking what's next? They had no time for an entire day of sadness when there were adventures to be had. Their constant desire to play beckoned me away from

my sadness. I would dry my tears, smile at their never ending quest for joy and go play with them. We made forts. We played superheroes. We blew bubbles outside and went for walks.

The children became my teachers, my healers and my therapists through play and love with the fresh, joyful energy they woke up with every day. Their energy for life was infectious and a reminder to me that every day we have a choice of what our experience is going to be, of how we are going to show up. Every day is a chance for new adventures. There is no concept of waiting when there are so many possibilities. In that way, they even reminded me of Mom. Mom had always had a childlike sense of play and wonder even as an adult. When I was around the children, their energy for life and adventure stirred that space inside of me as well. Every time I showed up for them, it helped me to show up for me again.

I love how kids embrace what is fun for them in the moment. I watch them bounce from activity to activity, like bees to flowers in the spring, and try to keep up with them when they are in the fast-lane of fun. There is no attachment to stop doing something that isn't fun anymore. What a wonderful luxury we don't often allow ourselves as adults. My adult approach at times has been I have put so much time in to this that I can't give up now. What if we didn't think of it as giving up? What would it create in our lives if we were willing to let go of what wasn't working for us anymore, from small things like a gym membership we never use to bigger things like a job or relationship. I wonder how much more joy we could have? How much fun could we have living from the space of unlimited creation where everything and anything is available to us?

I remember when Emma's 3rd birthday was coming up. I was curious about what she might want and asked her what she

would like for her birthday. She looked up toward the sky as she thought about it and then her face lit up with joy. She blurted out as much as I can get! I laughed at her response. What an amazing space to live from with no fear of asking for anything. Mom celebrated birthdays like that. She loved surprises and presents and birthdays. She always bought cards and small surprises for every holiday or simply because she felt like it. I have so many Snoopy cards from her telling her how much she loved me. She always made a big deal out of birthdays, others as well as hers. Her eyes sparkled with excitement on the big day and the more presents the better. What if as adults we asked with the enthusiasm of a child? What if we could never ask for enough from the universe and held the belief we could have it?

Somewhere as we grow up we start to notice or are told it is not a good thing to stand out or have too much or celebrate your brilliance. I wonder why and when that shift happens. Children constantly celebrate their accomplishments. They say "I did it!" or "I got it!" with smiles on their faces. Children enthusiastically celebrate even their smallest accomplishments and we gladly celebrate with them with high five's or hugs or spin them around in the air with love and encouragement. When do we become too old to celebrate ourselves? I wonder what would change in our world as big kids if we acknowledged our accomplishments, if we shared our successes without apology? What if we celebrated every accomplishment from that yummy, playful space children access so easily? Have you ever seen a child wearing their favorite outfit of the moment? There is no self-consciousness about them running around with a cape on. They may even have combined the costumes of their favorite superheroes and they do not care what anyone else thinks about them. They might be dressed in full princess regalia and proudly sashay by you in their sparkly princess heels. When do we decide it is better to strive for mediocrity

instead of standing out from the crowd? How much fun could we have celebrating our differences instead of trying to be like everyone else?

There is nothing that can compare to a welcome by children who are sooooo happy to see you. Six dark brown eyes shine with excitement when I walk in the door. I have arrived. "Carrie's here! Carrie's here!" Suddenly they race towards me, talking excitedly and all at once, telling me what they want to play. When they were younger they would run up and wrap their arms around my legs or put their arms up to be picked up. It is the best celebration. I imagine it is similar to receiving a standing ovation from a stadium filled with my biggest fans. It is one of the best things in the world. I would listen to their requests – racing game, superheroes, ice cream which were all games we had invented. Some of my favorite games we played together were food related. I remember us all sitting on the big couch in the living room and we would pretend one end was an ice cream stand. Chris or Cooper would take turns being the ice cream man. We would each place our orders, chocolate with sprinkles or strawberry swirl, and hand over pretend money. Another fun game we came up with was when Chris was first learning to write his letters in kindergarten. He needed to practice his letters, but he did not like sitting down and writing the same letter over and over again. I thought he might have more fun if he created a menu as a way to practice his letters. I helped him spell words to create the menu. He was very proud of his hand-written menu. We could choose from a peanut butter and jelly sandwich, a hamburger, spaghetti, chicken nuggets, and fries. We would give him our orders and then Cooper would be the cook and put it together and bring it to us. They also had pretend plastic food and a small kitchen and sometimes Cooper would "cook" us meals while Emma and I watched Chris play video games. It was fun for me to create new games for us to play together.

The Energy of Play

The Power of Play is watching movies over and over again and never growing tired of it, like *Despicable Me 2*. We have seen that movie so many times that we know it by heart. We repeat our favorite phrases during the movie. We laugh and play while we watch, waiting for our next favorite line. We jump up and shout "lipstick taser" when Lucy kidnaps Gru. We know the exact moment when Gru will trip the booby trap and Lucy say's "Ha, booby!" We stand up at the end of the movie and pretend we are shooting the jelly guns that transform the evil, purple minions back into the little yellow guys we love.

Chris and Cooper are in school now and Emma will soon follow. The one constant in life is change, nothing stays the same forever. Change can be scary, even when we know it is coming, if we let it be. It used to scare me when I thought about the children growing up and losing the playmates I had come to depend on. I do not have to lose them though. I realize there will be adventures we will all want to explore. Children seem to embrace change so easily, to relish it even. I would like to be an example for them to embrace change even when they do not know what it will bring them. I would like them to step into the change with the same enthusiasm and excitement they have now. What if the most uncomfortable changes for us, became the most rewarding?

What if the power of play was simply the power to be ourselves and have fun? I believe we appreciate so much in children what we judge in ourselves as adults - their sense of adventure, their enthusiasm to try new things, their quest to learn, their playful spirits, their belief in infinite possibilities. What would we be doing if we weren't judging ourselves? What if we lived every moment from the space of enthusiasm and adventure? Children show up every day. They keep going for it. Being a nanny has shown me the power of play. I keep a bag in my car that has bubbles, markers, sidewalk chalk, a magic wand,

and bouncy balls. I have dum-dum suckers and chocolate for real emergencies. This bag is for me just as much as for Chris, Cooper and Emma. I like to sit in the park and blow bubbles just as much as the kids do. I am choosing more and more from the energetic space of play, enthusiasm, joy and possibilities the little people in my life have shown me. I have recaptured that playful energy for myself and I invite you to do the same. I wonder what the energies of play could expand in your life?

Carrie Seela

Carrie Seela chooses to create her life from a place of having more fun, more joy and more of her. She enjoys being a playmate in the world with children and adults alike. She loves travel and her travels have allowed her to spend significant time in Costa Rica and Italy. Carrie is always on the lookout for new places to visit and people to play with. She loves playing with the energies of question and possibility and what's next?

Connect with Carrie at Facebook at Carrie Seela.

5

Playmates in the Strangest Places

ASHLEY MCCAUGHEY

Looking back on my childhood, I don't recall a lot of play that went on in my world. My Dad farmed and had cattle so there was always a lot to get done every winter, spring, summer and fall. I was also a big sister and my Dad's interesting point of view was that the oldest child was to look after the younger siblings… Thank God my parents only choose one more after me. My parents were young when they married and a short time later I choose to join them than two years later my sister, they chose some hard stuff before I was five, there was some heavy shit in that house! My parents weren't choosing to play either……they were too busy making sure that there was enough food on the table and clothes for their two little girls.

And not that they didn't choose play it just wasn't that often and the crazy thing is now with all the amazing Access Consciousness tools and choosing my awareness, I know that play follows joy, and money follows joy! So how much play are you refusing in your life that if you would choose it would give you all the money that you have ever desired?!

How much kindness is there in play?! As I reached adolescence there were always children around, I always loved their round cheeks, their small hands and all their curiosity. They seemed to be aware of how much gratitude I had for all their wonderment and questions. How much joy it brought me to play with them whether that was a game of "please chase me" or just listening to them talk and being totally present with every word that came from there sweet lips. It amazes me that a lot of these children have now grown into adults, and they have never forgotten the kindness that I had shown them. WOW can you say an AHAH moment, I have never actually acknowledged the gift that I BE to children!!!! Where in your life are you the gift of play?! And if you acknowledged it, what would your life be like?!

My parents choose to separate when I was 17, at no point in a child's life is that ever ease. With the tools of Access I have come to see all the gifts that, that one choice has brought to my life. I was eighteen years old when my sweet little brother Sam was born and 19 years old my sweet little brother Isaac was born. As you all read earlier that there wasn't a lot of play in my world as a child, well you can just imagine the play that occurred in my world once those little boys chose to join my family. I remember an afternoon at Grandma's where all we choose was to play! I'm not sure who was having more fun, my little brothers laughing at their big sisters or the big sisters laughing at their little brothers. Is there a child in your life that is that much of an invitation to play?! Are you a parent and all the everyday hustle and bustle of this reality has you NOT choosing to have all the laughter, joy and play that those amazing little beings are choosing?! Would you be willing to slow down and play for 10 minutes a day?! Instead of making those lunches for the next day or sweeping the floor because

The Energy of Play

you have company coming over?! Would you be willing to play with your child?! What if the play you choose with them is as much of a gift to them as it is to you?!

I am aware that there are many people out there that have chosen not to have children, me being one of them. These little infinite beings fascinate me, they don't have points of view, or judgment about anything that they choose. They don't stack the building blocks perfectly, or color in the lines, there is no form or structure to how they choose to play. Can you get a sense of how you played as a child?! What if that was actually how you created the life that you desired right now?! Are you playing in a small sand box when you could be playing in a sand box as big as the whole universe?! Would you choose greater for you now?!

As a little girl, who was really aware and so kind, an adult who choose to be kind to me, whether that was a hug or just to acknowledge me I was so grateful for. As there were many people in my universe that thought that children should not be heard or seen, so when an adult choose that kindness with me my whole universe changed and shifted. Would you treat little children as you should have been treated instead of how you were treated?!

Where are you choosing to play in your life?! Are you avoiding play?! What if adding some play in your world would bring you more joy and ease?! You have to get what play is for you and where you can add it to your life.

Animals have been an amazing source of play in my life, I am owned by a heeler cross who chooses to play on a regular basis whether that is chasing the cat, demanding a game of fetch or digging up a mole hill to locate the little creature. He is such an invitation! He even chooses to sing his little heart with me in the truck. What invitation of play are you refusing that if you would choose it would give you all of you?!

As a child and as an adult I have had the honor of having horses in my life. I rode at a very young age and was a natural! The second horse that owned me Bill, my Dad rode him first then he gave Bill to me to ride. Years before when I was two years old I gave Bill his name as my Dad hadn't given him one yet, Bill had my attention from that moment on. That little buckskin gelding had a lot to do with choosing me. That horse was fast and athletic, he would prance everywhere he went, and his favorite thing in the world was to chase cattle, or maybe it was running around the pasture as I was attempting to catch him to go on our next adventure. That refusing to be caught was a HUGE invitation to play I just never understood it until recently and a little bit of "Look how pretty I am?!" game. He would get you where you needed to be every time. I remember riding him and knowing that he loved that I was on his back and we were going to play. He had all the heart in the world, and he loved to run just as much as I loved to let him run.

In the summer time, Monday were always my favorite day, another day with my amazing play mate Bill. We would head to the farm, catch our horses and head to the neighbors to do a little pasture checking. We went rain or shine, windy or even if it was snowing, (yes, if it gets cold enough in the summer time it snows in Alberta, Canada) us kids would spot a coyote and race as fast as our horses would carry us to chase that mongrel away, the whole time giggling. We would talk about it later in the day and laugh some more about how one of us almost got that damn coyote. This was all playing, the joy and the giggles and the fun.

I was a serious child and teenager, I was more like a little old lady then I was a little girl. As I grew I became awkward in my own body, the curves started to show themselves where they were never before. My amazing horse would carry me to all the places where we were playing and Bill had no point of view about the curves that were now there. There was a calmness when I was with my horse, were all those insecurities dissipated. I could be all of me and play and giggle even when I didn't think that a single person saw the gift that I was, I was aware my horse felt differently.

There is no feeling in the world quite like you and your horse racing across the earth as you play together. He carried me over mountains, through streams and rivers, he ran sideways, he ran fast, chased cows and he jumped logs with me on his back, he was one of the greatest play mates that I was honored to have by my side. We danced around the show ring for a couple of years, this was not his favorite thing to do with me but Bill did it because I asked him too. And the amazing part is that I have never acknowledged the gift of play the horses that have been in my life were and are AND the gift of play that I was in there lives. WOW now what is possible?! Where have you been the gift of PLAY in your life?! I wonder if acknowledging it would allow more of it to show up?!

All that seriousness I was choosing as a child, I may have brought it with me into adulthood... how I chose to find a playmate. Interesting choice really, looking back at the playmates that I chose they were all serious men, with so much work in their universes, there wasn't a lot of time for play. These relationships never worked out for many reasons, a couple of them being that there was no playing, not with giggles, not with bodies, and not with kindness. With the tools of Access and attending classes all over the world all those points of view dissipated, and on a cold December evening there stood a man. His energy was different, there was a kindness and playfulness to him that I had never perceived before. I had been asking questions like crazy, asking the universe to show me something different, someone that would be a contribution to my life and living. And as if by magic there he was, my not so significant other. How does it get any better than that?! What if asking for a playmate to show up was a contribution to your life? What if the play that you both share can be an invitation for more joy, more ease and more money to show up in your life? But whatever you do, don't ask the universe to assist in bringing you a playmate that would add more to your life and living!!!

By sharing these stories, I hope that you can see that PLAY can be different for all of us, and maybe there is some play that you are choosing RIGHT NOW that you have not yet acknowledged. Please acknowledge it!!! The more you acknowledge that you are actually choosing it, the more you can have it in your life, followed by more joy, and way more fun! We didn't choose to come here and work our asses off, and to barely get by. What if you could ask money to come and play with you?! Instead of money just paying all your bills… What if you could invite money to come and play with you to create the life and living that you desire?!

What I am choosing to be aware of more and more every day is that when we chose to play, we are choosing more of who we be. We have been ingrained our whole entire lives that we have to take things seriously we have to be responsible adults in society and get things done and go to our jobs and get all our tasks done on time. How many times do we stop ourselves from being silly, dancing and moving our bodies, all forms of play with our bodies?! And what if that was all BULL SHIT?!? What if we have it all wrong?! What if the little children, the animals, and the playmates in our lives have a better idea as to what is going to create more in our life and living?!

Consider this your invitation… Where in your life could you add some play?! Just ask the question, remember it never shows up how you think it will.

About the Author

Ashley McCaughey

Ashley McCaughey was born and raised in Alberta, Canada. In a small rural community where animals and play were in abundance, she was aware at a young age that there was a different possibility with every aspect in her life.

After attending an Access Consciousness BARS class in August of 2012, those possibilities became a reality. She is still attending Access Consciousness classes all over the world. One her many targets is to become an Access Consciousness Certified Facilitator to continue to change the world.

Ashley is a BARS Facilitator and Practitioner as well as an ESSE Horse Practitioner, assisting to create different possibilities with horses and people. Ashley has recently become a Conscious Horse Conscious Rider Facilitator, where she shares more Access Consciousness tools in a two-day class that empowers the horse and rider. Check out Ashley's website at www.TheJoyOfYou.com.

CHAPTER

6

Playing with the Light

Dr. Lisa Cooney

"Every day you play with the light of the universe."

~Pablo Neruda

Life can be much simpler – and way more fun – than most of us make it out to be.

So simple in fact that, for the most part, my entire 25 years of working in non-traditional and energetic therapies boils down to one major theme: Find out what's *not* working for people, empower a better choice, contribute to the actualization of their desire and generate the multiple possibilities of creating their desired life.

When I do this, the results are stunning.

And it isn't just that they're happier, though they are that. It's also

that whatever the "issue" is – as indicated by the medications they're on, the diseases they have, the lack of money, or something else – also goes away. *Poof!* Like magic… and all that's required for achieving these results is the willingness to choose for yourself and bring the energy and demand of play into your life. So why aren't more people doing it?

That's a very good question…

What I've found in my work is that most people with a history of abuse have a difficult time playing, having fun, and letting go. It's not that they don't have the ability – we all do – it's that play, in their minds, has become associated with something entirely different – and "bad."

For example, sometimes play turned into sexual activity where something feels wrong but good at the same time. It's confusing because you're not really sure what's wrong, what's right, or what's going on. In this scenario, play becomes associated with sexual shame, a sense of wrongness that says, "I shouldn't be doing this," and anything that resembles it – fun, looseness, lightness – equates to feeling out of control, similar to what you felt like when you were being abused.

In real play, you're engaging in an activity for enjoyment and recreation, inviting something new to exist through imagination, activity, possibility, generation and creation.

With abuse, play changes. It becomes serious and practical, all about "what's going to happen," which then constricts – cutting off the freedom and awareness to just frolic, like a child running around free.

When you're a child, you don't have thoughts that worry and wonder if something bad is going to happen again. Few things are more fun than the element of the unknown, the anticipation, the surprise. What child hasn't eagerly asked the question, "Did you bring me a surprise?" and clapped their hands with delight and expectation? On the other hand, to someone who has an abusive past, surprise is the last thing they want. Hypervigilance becomes the watchword. And looking behind your back or around the corner becomes the game of survival.

The Robber Baron of Play

With abuse, you get locked down in having to hold your body a certain way, constricting yourself a certain way, doing things a certain way, so you don't encounter abuse again. You go into the energy of conclusion, decision, judgment, and restriction. Like a bad case of arthritis, you become so rigid that you walk yourself out of any creativity, generation, and fluidity. You're stuck in what I call *the invisible cage of abuse*, which I describe fully in my book, *Kick Abuse in the Caboose*, soon to be released.

In this self-imposed cage, you can't have any fun because you're always waiting for the next catastrophe to occur. Navigating life becomes somewhat like rafting through white water rapids. In this state, you wonder, "Why does this keep happening to me? Everything's such a struggle. Nothing ever works for me no matter how hard I try. Why is everything so hard?" The answer is that, essentially, you're locked in the four "pillars," or the four "D's," that make up the invisible cage: **D**issociation, **D**enial, **D**efense, and **D**isconnection.

In this stance towards life, even the simplest creative activities, such as hiking by yourself can be rendered off limits because you're too acutely aware of yourself in a world that has become a dangerous place. Constantly on guard, aware that at any time your safety or comfort can be interrupted, it spreads to other aspects of your being. It's everywhere – in your body, relationships, money, sexualness – constricting and contracting

instead of expanding into new possibility.

From a health standpoint, rigidity and lockdown in your body can have serious repercussions. Without a fluid, free-flowing form, blockage can ensue, literally constricting the blood flow, depriving your organs of oxygen and other vital elements your body requires to function effortlessly. Over time, this can further deteriorate into chronic conditions or possibly adrenal or endocrine disorders easily. It certainly did for me.

With relationships, you may tend to choose people who are more indicative of the lockdown that's present and stuck in your body because that's how you know, or think, relationships should be. You energetically choose people, consciously or unconsciously, that constrict you rather than those who create possibility for and with you. Even your income and potential to earn money is at risk because of your need to play it safe. An example would be taking a job you don't really like but that gives you a salary you can count on, even though you hate going to it every day. Where's the fun in that choice?

It's like living backwards, against the energy instead of moving forward with possibility. Life becomes "How safe am I?" instead of "How amazing! What else can I create?"

Play and creativity are fueled with imagination, a mind that is open and questioning, a relaxed space, and the possibility of something generative and expansive occurring. These are quite the opposite of what happens when your mind is held captive in the invisible cage of abuse:
- High need for structure
- Controlling
- Prepared for anything
- Need to know it all
- Withdrawn and Isolated

- Conclusion-oriented
- Conforming
- Mistrust of the unknown
- Unsafe
- Hyper-vigilant awareness

Your creative forces are kept flowing by tapping into the molecular energetics of the freewheeling knowingness of pure possibility – one where anything is possible and communion is the source of creation.

In play, there are a lot of unknowns and how does it get any better than that? You *get* to create everything and anything you desire. Yet, if you experienced any form of abuse, that "unknown" quality could trigger fear and destroy creation.

Radical and Orgasmic Aliveness

Have you ever noticed how long children stay with something? They just move from one thing to the next thing – mind and body together – fully present in the moment. They choose their next moment based on what's fun and exciting.

In my work, I refer to this as *full radical and orgasmic aliveness,* where your whole being is present with everything that you're doing. You're not worrying about the future, paying your bills, or how you look, and there's a great sense of fun and play in just being present.

With abusive situations, you don't want to be there at all.

Orgasm isn't just about sex… it's about sensual, embodied pleasure. What if you want to smell a rose, or buy roses for yourself to have beautiful color in your house? What if you want to put strawberries on your granola and just the taste of it is was orgasmic and delicious? That's fun and orgasmic!

Kids don't have preconceived ideas; they haven't developed the notions that we've learned as adults that constrict us and keep us from embodying full pleasure.

And, if you don't want to be in your body, how do you think that affects, say, a relationship that *is* sexual and sensual? It's hard to have a desirable and orgasmic sexual relationship when you're so used to abandoning your body in order to not feel what you didn't want in the first place.

What, then, can you do to bring yourself fully into your body… and fully into play?

Two Steps into Play

When you were growing up, were you ever told to ask yourself, "Am I having fun right now?" For most adults, choosing for the fun of it is a foreign concept, hardly a choice at all. If you've never been in your body, you've also probably never given yourself the choice to ask and demand for yourself. Would you even know what question to ask?

The first step to play is to simply become aware that something isn't working for you and give yourself the allowance to say, "I don't really know what's going on here, but something doesn't feel right and I choose to make a change, even if I don't know what to ask." Just that awareness will bring you present to yourself.

The next step is to ask questions that invoke the energy of play such as:

- Body, is this fun for me?
- Am I having fun right now?
- Am I learning something?
- Is this expanding my reality?

- Am I grateful?
- Am I enjoying what I'm being right now?
- Is this person receiving me?
- Am I able to receive?
- Does my body feel good?
- What else is possible here?
- Can I do whatever I want?
- Am I living my fun-filled, play-filled reality?
- What else could I choose that would be more playful?

The energy of play isn't about doing what was fun as a kid – it's the *spirit of fun* and the playground of possibility you had then in the now. It's about what can you do to create a new possibility and get out of the constriction every day.

For example, I could sit in front of my computer all day mailing things out and responding to people, but that's not really fun for me. What's more fun is doing the energy work, the Voice of America radio show, writing these chapters, and talking with people, creating possibility. But there was a long time in my own life where play became unsafe, and I was more rigid and better with form and structure. If anything upset that, I'd get freaked out. Now I barely have a structure. I just go with the energy of "what is" and what is required of me each day.

This is what we do as kids. We just go with the energy of what's possible today. When abuse occurs, innocent freedom and your playground of possibility gets all locked up, limited, and constricted. Fortunately, there is a way back.

Light is Right

What's fun for people is what's *light* for them; it's something you can feel in your body. Lightness is like the truth – because the most expansive, joyful thing you like doing lightens everyone. You're more fun for *all* of us.

The energy of play is about discovering what your fun reality is – emotionally, financially, relationally, sexually, and otherwise – by asking, "Body, what would you like to do today? Who would you like to be with? Who would you like to sleep with? What would you like to eat? What would you like to create? What part of your business requires your attention today?"

If my body tells me, "Let's go to the gym," and I don't go, it gets really unhappy. Going to the gym can be a form of play, moving the spirit and energy. Or if it says, "Eat this," and I eat something else, I'm overriding it. The whole idea is to listen to your body, to the whispers your body is telling you about what it requires each day – and what you require each day – and going forward with it.

You can bring this energy of play into all your decisions of what's right for you. How? Well, what's fun for you? Do that!

What's Fun for You Is Play!

It's what makes you work through the day without eating and then suddenly look up and think, "Oh, wow, I haven't eaten!" You're having fun because you're really into what you're doing. You're living off the energy just as children do, who continually need reminding, "You have to eat now... you've got to go to bed now." They're in the moment with a freedom you have to walk them out of.

Usually adults have to relearn what light or heavy feels like so that, when presented with choice, they know it in their body. Where there's been abuse, your energy is infiltrated, your space is violated, and your consciousness is anesthetized. With all of that happening, how could you know what's light and right for you? You only know what is suffering and bad for you. Abuse takes your whole view of life and twists it to be more dangerous and not so fun.

The Energy of Play

Becoming aware of what's light and right for you allows you to create what's fun for you. It's like redefining your molecules to what they knew before they were abused. If it feels light and expansive and bubbly, go for it. If it's heavy and dense, ask more questions and don't choose it until lightness exists. Unfortunately, too many of us choose the heavy and dense and not the light, and that's how we wake up in psychiatry offices waiting for medication.

Just remember…

What's Light is Right

The fun is in being a demand *for yourself*, like children who just go with, "Hey, let's do this!" and, "Hey, let's do that!" Of course, as adults, there's a little more pragmatic nature to it, but if you embody the energy of play I'm talking about here, you'll engage your generative, creative imagination. It's the childlike innocence that's in all of us, which lives within our bodies no matter what age we are.

And it's as easy as choosing to be fully present doing what works for you – right now – in the most light and expansive way.

10-Second Increments

Especially when starting out, the "Light and Heavy" tool is particularly effective when you do it combined with choosing in 10-second increments. This means you make a choice 10 seconds at time, giving yourself the freedom to change your mind and tuning in to what is most true for you in any moment. That's play.

The beauty of 10 seconds is two-fold: 1) you tap into more freedom and 2) discover more intimacy with yourself. If you

choose something and it doesn't work for you, then in the next 10 seconds you choose again. Each choice gives you an awareness of what works for you, keeping in mind that what worked for you yesterday may not work for you next week, or what worked for you an hour ago may not work for you now.

If you've never lived in 10-second increments, as you can imagine, you go back and forth between freedom and constriction pretty regularly. But, we're only looking for one degree of shift to make a change. Like a muscle, you build on it.

Sometimes I'm asked how purpose figures into this. Well, if you're choosing in 10-second increments, you can't really get locked into much of a purpose. It's more about pleasure, knowing that living a joyous, playful life creates happiness – and I would propose that happiness and consciousness are the biggest targets we have on this planet.

Think about how many happy people you know. Have you ever noticed that everything seems to come to them with ease, joy and glory?

When I'm happy, everything works. When I'm in my play-filled energy, I only focus on expansion and possibility. I'm just here enjoying every moment on this planet as a new possibility of generation and creation for a brand new reality – one that breeds joy, pleasure, possibility, play, and happiness. That's quite a different reality than someone who's been abused and thinks, "Everything's so hard and, no matter how much I do or hard I try, nothing ever changes for me."

Play Is Pragmatic

...find what is most interesting to you. The more you learn, the more you want to learn. It is fun.
~ Warren Buffett

The Energy of Play

The energy of play isn't only fun – it's also pragmatic. It's certainly worked for Warren Buffett who, in *Tap Dancing to Work* by Carol Loomis, is described as motivated by having fun, not making money. And I've had many clients leave jobs for something they really love and, when they do, make three or four times the amount they did before.

When your body tells you what it wants and you do it, what shows up in your life becomes more easy and fun-filled. By listening to what's right for you and bringing that forward, you're conspiring with the universe to make your life *easier* – all because you're doing what's fun for you.

Conversely, if something's not working for you, you eliminate it from your reality. This doesn't mean not paying your bills, but rather finding another, more fun and joyous way to take care of things.

For example, I have my bills on an automatic payment plan with my bank because it's not fun for me to spend time figuring it out each month. Knowing it's handled every day, every month – that's fun for me and when I have created beyond the payments I pay it off. I like never having to worry about being late with anything; that's not where I desire to put my attention. I'd rather put it on creating a new possibility and, if that's something beyond what I currently have, I know I have free choice to go and create the extra money for it.

The Bridge to Radical Aliveness

As the catalyst of the "Beyond Abuse Revolution," the target is to eradicate all forms of abuse off this planet through two overarching methods: identifying the invisible cage of abuse and directing people to cross the "bridge" to radical aliveness. Radical Aliveness is made up of four components, or "4 C's": **Choosing for you, Committing to you, Collaborating**

and knowing that the universe is conspiring to bless you, and Creating the life you desire. Radical Aliveness is fun!

You cross this bridge when you enter into the spirit of play and choose what's fun for you. *The whole goal in the energy of play is to put yourself first.*

If you're not used to doing this, then the idea of choosing for you is going to be a radically new perspective. For sure, people who have been abused are the most confounded by this notion because they put everybody else first – they don't exist.

Play acts to reclaim your freedom of expression.

Beyond intentions and goals, learning to choose for you from the energy of play will open you to possibility in every moment, and bring you back into communion with all life at a whole new level of ease, joy and glory.

"What would your life be like if you were willing to be its catalyst?"

To access your *Free Gifts*, go to: www.DrLisaCooney.com.

About the Author

Dr. Lisa Cooney

Dr. Lisa Cooney, licensed Marriage and Family Therapist, Master Theta Healer, certified Access Consciousness Facilitator, is the creator of *Live Your ROAR! Be You! Beyond Anything! Creating Magic!*

An internationally recognized expert, Dr. Lisa brings an *"I'm Having It! ...No Matter What!"* approach to everything she does and teaches people how to playfully engage this magical and generative energy for creating a life that's light and right and fun for them.

Having transformed her own life from abuse and loss to a virtual playground of wonder and joy, Dr. Lisa generously shares her gifts and creative tools for transformation. She invites and guides others beyond all obstacles into a place of their own knowing… that space where they have direct access to the whisperings of consciousness.

"Are you ready to *ROAR* – to live your own Radical Orgasmic Alive Reality –*Beyond Anything* you've ever imagined?"

To contact her or to learn more about Live Your ROAR, LLC: http://drlisacooney.com/about-dr-lisa/.

7

Getting to Playful

Erica Glessing

Being playful is easy, especially if you are a kitten, or a puppy, or a young person. Being playful and the play inherent in a human being is something that can be gone in an instant, shattered in the choices we make or the pain we experience.

I like to have joyful exuberance and how do I get there? How do I get to playful?

It's a taking time away from the worry, it's a way of being where I don't know what's going to happen next. It's a looking around the corner at what might be, at what I haven't dreamed of yet, and it comes to me when I wake up dreams that I left hiding.

Sometimes I wonder when it will all work out, when my life will flow like the river, and when I will be in that space of nirvana I associate with joy.

Then I look around and say to myself how did I ever get so lucky, I have a great place to live, and fun people to work with, and I have work in the world that brings joy to people -- plus three children I love beyond life -- and a man who is the sweetest man in the world. So if I'm not going to be playful now, when?

The Power of Laughter to Heal

I am curious about the energy of laughter and the power of laughter to heal. I was a psychology major in college, and I was always jumping into physiology, since social psychology basically concluded that human behavior couldn't be predicted.

So I jumped into the study of the body only to learn -- guess what? -- the body can't be predicted either! Physiology, when it gets deep, is also a mystery to science, and the science of it is always uncovering new mysteries and new truths that change all beliefs before it.

So when you get playful with the body and healing, you can change that which maybe you thought you could not change. You can in an instant be healed, a beam of light, a laser focus, and change shows up BAM like you don't even know what happened.

Then laughter heals, and laughter shifts your way of being into a new way of being, and the more laughter you can experience the more healing your cells will experience.

Begin by looking at this:

    What makes you happy?
    What gives you joy?
    What changes your chemistry so you feel good?
    What changes your energy into brightness?

The Energy of Play

These are steps you can take into playfulness for you. It's a discovery of you, and what gives you a zing or a lot of woo hoo. One of my friends likes shoes (a lot) she has a closet full of shoes maybe each pair worth hundreds of dollars. I can't get that energized about shoes, I have a few sandals and a few boots, shoes aren't my thing. I like animals, warm and furry, horses, kittens, dogs, maybe an occasional bird. I like to talk to animals and they like to talk to me. So for me, my favorites in the world are babies, children, animals, and a great game of basketball on TV. Those are the things that rock my boat. Then, next, I like listening to RNB music like Anita Baker, and Luther Vandross, and that sweet sound of music that warms up my soul all the way down to my toes.

No one outside of you can tell you exactly what takes you into that space of joyful appreciation.

When I am looking for playful inspiration, I drive to the beach and soak in the energy of the waves crashing upon the shore. I was at the beach twice in the last week. Living in California, I do my best not to deprive myself of these things.

Toxic People

One of the questions I am asked possibly the most, around happiness, relates to being around people who complain, or people who yell at you, or people who find fault with you. So maybe you wake up playful, and then someone takes you out of your joy.

Parents and spouses and siblings and ex-spouses frequently have this role in your life. You somehow gave them the key to bring you down a notch. Maybe you were too happy, or too much fun, or too joyful, and they could not comprehend this. So you let them call you names or say other things that turned your joy into something less.

I'm always surprised by the ways adult parents choose to manipulate and bring down adult children. I'm surprised by how I let my ex bring me down. So what do we do when this shows up?

I have become deft at moving quickly from the space of those who can't see light. If their world is so dark and impermeable that my light is a threat, I let it go.

Let it go.

Let them go.

Let go of the drama.

Let go of the names they call you.

Let go of any need to justify, or villify, or categorize, or qualify, or explain the behavior of another.

I move away from the space of those whose darkness gives their lives bleakness. Even last week I noticed someone in my space was spending a lot of time talking about others in a mean-ish way. I chose at that instant to stay away from that person, why would I want to be in the space of her thoughts and her comments?

It's a constant discipline sometimes to clear the beliefs of others from my head. It's funny how quickly their thoughts and beliefs can jump back in.

Another tool I use is to expand my energy when others might desire that I contract my energy. I practice expanding my energy. Making my energy as big as my room, my house, my city, my country, the universe, and then as big as all the planets.

Then I see the person, and I ask myself to expand even bigger, again.

I even practice driving up to say a place where people are that sometimes trigger me standing on my head and acting like a smaller pitiful being. And I expand my energy again, and again, and again.

Yes, you guessed it. Usually the person walks away or disappears. It's not that fun for them to be around me when I'm in my brilliance. So if someone walks away from you, it just might be they aren't happy and don't desire to be happy, and your joy isn't that fun for them (yet). Keep being it though, because they might seek you out at some point when they desire to shift.

So being joyful and playful when others are marose -- well, you might stand out a bit. I just keep choosing to be silly when the situation doesn't call for it. Even death doesn't make me cringe so much. I know the spirit is on the other side and will probably have a lot to say in the days and years to come -- I can't get too drawn into any of that. I figure when I die no one will take it that seriously because I didn't, and don't.

I guess if you are still hungry for tools to let go of noxious toxic people here are a few more:

Why am I letting someone outside of me keep me small?

How much time am I willing to spend processing someone else's stuff each day?

Will I get where I choose to go faster if I am jumping into their cesspool or if I am letting them be in their cesspool by themselves?

Am I willing to trust that each person gets to experience whatever they choose to experience? That includes me, so am I willing to jump into joy for no reason, right now?

Julie Andrews sang it best in the movie *The Sound of Music*. "Raindrops on roses and whiskers on kittens, doorbells and sleighbells and warm woolen mittens... these are a few of my favorite things..."

Do yourself this favor today and get closer to your favorite things, and enjoy and appreciate the people you love. It can all be gone, in an instant, and you won't look back and say "I wish I hadn't been so happy."

When you aren't sure, be careful not to define happy the way someone else defines happy. One of my friends called me once for help with her happiness. She said, "Erica, I don't get this!" and I knew her quite well. And I asked her how she is when she is planting flowers in front of her house. And that gives her so much calm joy. And she said, "Oh yes, but that is a calm joy," and I said yes, does that give you peace? And she said yes, and we knew, right then, that this was her happy. So know that it is your happy, not someone else's, that matters for you.

Go now, and play!

About the Author

Erica Glessing

Erica Glessing is a dreamer, a creative, a bright spirit who laughs easily and often. She is the CEO of Happy Publishing, joyful to have generated #1 bestselling author status for more than 130 authors to date. Who knows what she will be up to next! She's also the host of **The Erica Glessing Show**, on YouTube and a podcast.

You can find Erica here:

www.HappyPublishing.net
www.EricaGlessing.com
on Facebook @happinessquotations
on Twitter @ericaglessing
on YouTube @ Erica Glessing
on Podbean @The Erica Glessing Show
on Amazon @Erica Glessing

8

What Does PLAY Mean to You?

SUSAN SHATZER

Perhaps you think playing is something only children do or maybe playing only happens on vacations at your house. What if you took a moment and traveled back in time to a place where you remember playing was fun? I mean specifically a time when you were having a ton of fun, a full out, best day ever, laughter filled moments, possibly even one labeled "The Good Ol' Days." How many months, years or even decades did that memory take you back? Did your mind immediately become flooded with many joyous playgrounds you used to visit, family gatherings you would look forward to attending, local parks with friends on weekends, church functions with great food after services, or many other flashes and pictures of times long past? Did you find yourself smiling or even laughing at these times as you recalled where you were, who you were with and what you were doing? I know I did! What if there is a youthfulness and generative component to the Energy of Play? Could the more playing one does, increase the level of joy in

their life or even give someone a reason to live?

For me, playing began all over again since my college days with an even greater commitment to the cause of creating youthful generative playful energy as often as possible when my son, Nicholas, was born. Up until that point, I had a completely "Play less" life. I had fallen into the adult, very serious, too many responsibilities; have to get up early in the morning, doing what I was supposed to do because it was the right thing to do because that is what was expected of me to do and so on. One particular day especially pops out for me and I chuckle each time I think of it. It is a precious event that I'll never forget. In fact, I remember all the glorious details due to a completely new level of play that was achieved and created much joy for everyone.

I picked up Nicholas from Kindergarten on a very rainy afternoon in Florida. As we exited the building and began to walk through the parking lot, we were required to dodge cars waiting in line to pick up their children. Nicholas unexpectedly stopped abruptly at the very edge of a humungous puddle and yelled to me, "Mom," which immediately without hesitation got me to stop in my tracks. The look on his face said, do you dare me to do this? I swear I knew the question was coming as I headed over to him, flagging motorists to halt and answered "Yes Nicholas." Here it is, just as I suspected, "Can I jump?" I don't know about other moms and dads but a huge amount of judgment ran through my head. I began thinking I should say NO because your shoes will get wet and they'll never dry by tomorrow. And NO because you are holding up traffic and it's not fair to the other kids waiting for their parents to pick them up. And NO because what would these parents think of me allowing my child to stand in the rain, play in a puddle and hold up traffic. I know, incredibly crazy right? It was absolutely not like me to choose the complete opposite of what I was

The Energy of Play

thinking. I threw caution to the wind with my hand in the air motioning for the traffic to stop as I held his backpack and replied gleefully, "Yes, go for it!" Shocked with my response, he looked at me for confirmation and when he was sure he heard me correctly, he jumped and splashed and kicked the water. It was extremely rewarding for me having stopped traffic for his spur of the moment, must have it now playfulness, with all the ease and pure enjoyment of the adventure he just created. As the puddle was stomped, kicked, and splashed empty, Nicholas indicated he was done by taking my hand and slowly leading me toward our car while laughing and giggling about how much fun he had and asking if I had seen him splash the water all the way over to the edge of the sidewalk.

We were having so much fun playing together, I completely forgot about the other drivers waiting. As soon as we stepped clear of the cars, I thanked everyone waiting in line who had watched us stop to honor the energy of play with a silent thank you wave and was very surprised to see the reaction from each of the drivers as they passed. It was amazing how many smiles and thumbs up I received and not a single annoyed response. Wow!

It hadn't been about how many rules I was breaking or how many people might get angry for making them wait. It was about honoring a five-year-old's request to take time out of his busy schedule of rules and routines to simply play. Could it have been the joy, fun and playfulness of Nicholas that captured each of them in their own way? Maybe taking them back to their childhood where they were allowed to play in the face of doing the right thing because what would people think if they choose to play possibly creating joy, outside the box of this realities rules and regulations. Or could it have been simply they were smiling at what an interesting choice I made allowing him to dance and prance in a mud puddle as well as

how much time it would take me to get the mud off his clothes. It suddenly occurred to me as we arrived at the car, how many of those thoughts didn't even belong to me. As he climbed in his booster seat, I clicked his security belt and considered how many more times and ways can we parents choose ease, joy, and play that changes everyone's state of being. What if this created more fun and laughter in the world? Happy Parents + Happy Kids = a Happy Family for everyone to enjoy a Happy World!

As a kid, for me, growing up with people in my life who were worriers of magnitude was not much fun. My grandmother was the queen of worrying. She could win awards and prizes with the amount of sleep she lost by worrying about others. There always seemed to be something to fix, change, wasn't quite right, to look out for, or be careful of. She appeared to be locked in a perpetual cycle of; what if this happens, or that happens, doom and gloom. I knew there had to be another way to have a life with ease, joy, fun, laughter and play. There came a time in my life when I consciously decided, this was absolutely going to change not just for me and my clients but also for my son.

Nicholas and I started at a very young age, a nightly routine, to talk about all the ups and downs of the day which sometimes led back to the day before. One evening, I noticed he was beginning to mimic the people in his life and worry. I began to question what else I could do to shift and change this. I woke up the next morning with the awareness it might be fun and beneficial to teach Nicholas a mantra to use before going to sleep. That night, we created a game with remembering these four sentences. TODAY IS OVER! TOMORROW IS A NEW DAY! IT WILL BE A GREAT DAY! BECAUSE I CHOOSE! Amazingly these sentences gifted him the ability to let go of everything before going to sleep. It included the good and bad

parts of his day without judgment of it? Plus it gave him the freedom to toss away anything that was still bothering him by the end of the day? "No Carry Overs," I would say to him when he tried to hold on to something! It was my target to also empower him to choose what kind of day he was going to have the next morning before he even went to sleep the night before. Even today, most clients I work with have been entrained and engrained by family, friends, and society that there is a right and wrong way of being in the world which is actually not a kindness to them. Do you know there has to be something different than stress, worry, and sadness that might include ease, joy and play but you just don't know where to get it?

Nicholas and I continued saying this mantra together for years both in and out of school. It really gave him ease with not making himself good or bad or right or wrong but instead, allowing the day to be merely over and acknowledging that tomorrow was going to be a new day. It is truly a different way of being and living. It reset his preset from the energy of dwelling on the past which recreated the same thing over and over in his life. This was also true of the amazing and wonderful things he had done that day as well. All his grand slams, A grades, touchdowns, competition wins and for you bonuses received, raises acquired, successful company take-over's and more all go away at the end of the day. This mantra brought Nicholas to a place each morning where he focused on out creating himself. What if you had the possibility of creating what would actually work for you? The mantra was able to take any weight from the day off his shoulders every evening even the stuff that wasn't his got left behind. It is interesting how many of us worry for and about others? Are you a worrier? Do you worry about the things you have no control over? Is it a habit for you? Was worrying something you were taught by your school or your church? Or possibly if there is such a thing the worry gene was passed down to you by your mother or father? Who did you

learn it from? Let me ask you, does worrying actually work?

Nicholas and I were fortunate to have my parents and grandmother live with us for the winter each year in sunny Florida. I'd like to share with you an example of how powerful playing can be in one's life. Not too long ago, my grandmother, who was well into her 90s, decided it was her time to cross over. Not on my watch, I secretly thought to myself. One evening, very unexpectedly, her health began to drastically decline. My mother was instructed to have her DNR (do not resuscitate) letter available for emergency services. The letter was validated from another state which to my mother's surprise, made it illegal in Florida. My parents immediately left my grandmother in my care to acquire a valid DNR in the event it was needed that night. In the mean time, my son and I climbed in bed with her and began to talk about his day at school. We noticed she began to show interest by smiling in what Nicholas and I were talking about. It appeared to us that her state of weakness began to dissipate so we started to ask her questions about her schooling as a child. Eventually, she sat up and began telling us a story about the fun and joy of growing up as a young girl climbing the mountains with her mother to pick strawberries. Noticing that her condition was continuing to improve, I prepared a bowl of strawberries for the three of us to enjoy. She had us laughing about all the many different things she still recalled from her school days including the names of many of her friends. She even remembered her middle school theme song and sang it to us. Nicholas thought it might be a good idea to teach her his mantra because of how sad she appeared to be much earlier in the day. Being so excited to teach his great-grandmother something new, he spent time going over and over the four sentences with her. When we were just about finished practicing and with our snack, my parents walked in the door and froze in their tracks because they heard singing, giggling and laughter but couldn't believe it. They slowly approached her bedroom door as the three of us let out a huge roar of laughter. Shocked at her improvement as both my parents were that evening, she continued to bring joy into our lives and to play with us for another 5 years! When she became wheelchair bound, we would joke and play about how her chariot awaited her and would call her Cindy…short for Cinderella. When she became unable to lift her feet as the wheelchair rolled along, she would alert us to her missing shoe by mentioning that she had lost one of her glass slippers while dancing in the ballroom. At times, we would all play with her and refer to my father as her knight in shining armor coming to take her away as he pushed her wheelchair through the house and into her bedroom. She loved the warmth of being on the lanai so my mom and I would position her facing the sun and giggle like little school girls calling her Miss Hollywood by playing dress up the way we protected her with a hat, gave her a hand fan and really big sunglasses even though she had lost her sight many years earlier. We would schedule Christmas cookie decorating play dates for her with the grand kids. All year, they would talk about how excited they were about making plans together for the next cookie baking party. We would dangle delicate, extremely breakable, and exceptionally old, ornaments off her fingers after they were unwrapped to keep them safe while waiting for little fingers to place them on the tree. We truly laughed and played our way through those next 5 years. Could it have been the memories of her past adventures when she was a little girl? Or could it have been when Nicholas taught his great-grandmother the mantra and how to use it so as not to worry anymore? We will never know?

To this day, my parents still ask me what I did that night which created such a huge shift for her and I really don't have an answer. I do know that Nicholas and I have a different way of being together where we create our life without a point of view of playing and having fun. If it's not fun, we just fix it.

What Does PLAY mean to You? ~ Susan Shatzer

What if, kids today aren't buying into our worry, trauma, and drama lifestyle where we secretly wish we could be a kid again? Playing around or goofing off as some people call it, is a quick and easy way to inject a different lighter energy into your life. At what age were you when you gave up playing and having fun because you were told it was time to get serious? What if it has nothing to do with your age, occupation, or location but the energy of your playful spirit? And what if you have the choice to choose differently at any moment and when you do, you not only heal yourself but others around you? Have you ever just stopped fighting with your child and started laughing. The really intense laughing with watery eyes, bent over because it hurts so much, people stop and look at you funny kind of laughing. Try it some time, kids don't know what to think or say next and just start laughing too. What if life really was about how much fun you can have playing? I double dog dare you to choose differently and make that change!

About the Author

SUSAN SHATZER

Susan Shatzer is a 3x #1 Best Selling Author. She is as an International Facilitator for Consciousness and known as a "Consciousness Revolutionary". Susan has appeared on multiple TV networks such as the LifeStyle Channel, LA36, Access Sacramento, Can-TV Chicago and the CREATE-U Expert Series in NYC. Susan has a natural gift and talent for both TV and radio. She is a casting director for the "AskBONBON" international TV show and hosted the "Ask A Question Change Your Life" radio show. Susan has run a successful coaching business; became a Bars, Body, and Certified International Facilitator with Access Consciousness® and is now the CEO of From Creation to Cradle™, running quarterly global seminars on Conscious Birthing and Beyond.

#1 Best Selling Books include:
I'm Having It
The Energy of Spirit

Creations! Conscious Fertility and Conception, Pregnancy and Birth

Connect with Susan:
Facebook: https://www.facebook.com/susan.shatzer
Twitter: https://twitter.com/Susan_Shatzer

A Selection of Susan's Workshops and Events include:

* What If Getting Pregnant, Being Pregnant, and Giving Birth was Joyful?
* Roll-Up Your Judgment and Undress Yourself with Kindness!
* Having Money, Wealth and Abundance in Any Economy!
* What if money REALLY wasn't the problem, YOU ARE?
* 52 Body Processes to Change Your Body and Your Life!
* How to Become a Magnet for Money Now and in the Future?
* Ask A Question and Change Your Life on Purpose!
* What if we are the change the Earth requires?
* Magic! You are it! Be it with your Business!
* Stand and Command A Different Reality!
* Relationships and Parenting Made Easy!

9

Unsnuffing Your Playfulness

Janie Lin Smith

So I had to giggle right off the bat! Did you know that "unsnuffing" is not even a word? Spell check wanted to change it to unstuffing! How funny is that? What's really funny is that gave me an awesome awareness of how much people have stuffed and stifled and snuffed out who they are, and pretend to walk around this planet as "playful happy" people. Do you see that?

Have you ever gone to the park, or somewhere where there are lots of people and just watched them from the space of curiosity? What goes through your awareness? You may find that truly happy people are few and far between. So most of the time in parks you will see people jogging or walking their dogs or playing with their kids or watching their kids play and so on.

Can you perceive the messages their bodies are sending out? Can you perceive all the judgments of what the people think

they should and shouldn't be doing, and what they think is fun that actually isn't with them?

In this reality we have been taught to be very conclusion-oriented about EVERYTHING! For example, to be healthy, we are supposed to exercise this many times a week for this long, and eat only this kind of food, and drink only this certain stuff and bla, bla, bla.

Yes, there is the random person flying through the park and you can perceive their body going "YES!!!" and you see the person smiling even though they can't breathe, and it's fun and exhilarating for them, and you know that. Like there's no doubt that's one of the things that person and their body truly enjoys in their life.

Then you see the other person that's there running through the park and you can perceive their feet like lead bricks, and their muscles tense and sore, and their lungs painfully gasping for air. You can perceive this person pushing their body through their planned out course because "this is supposed to be good for them and they will at some point feel good if they just keep going."

Oh My! That's exhausting just perceiving that!

So anywhere in there are there any questions? Not so much. Mostly just all conclusions. Do you suppose if the person pushing their body through the park at a dead run, had asked their body if it would like to jog through the park and if that would be fun, and say they were open to receiving messages from their body, do you suppose they would have still gone trotting through the park? Do you suppose they would continue to choose more pain and suffering?

The Energy of Play

Isn't that funny? We buy into all this stuff, and then do these things that other people "seem to enjoy," and wonder why it doesn't seem to work the same way for us.

So this is where I used to function. I would buy into what I was told would or should work or what should be fun and what play was supposed to be and look like so much that I really couldn't have told you who I was, let alone even make choices or decisions without having them totally validated and approved. Then I would go into major wrongness and self-judgment and even into depression and total unawareness, because of course not everyone is the same, has the same targets, and desires the same things in their life.

A few years ago I was introduced to Access Consciousness®. From attending my first Bars class to Certified Facilitators class, and the many additional classes I have attended since, has truly created a life of choice. Functioning now from being, knowing, perceiving and receiving instead of thoughts, feelings and emotions that weren't even mine is what creates the space of ease and play for me.

Prior to being introduced to Access Consciousness, I had looked to Reiki for some enlightenment. I became a Reiki Master. It was like the door had been cracked opened for a whole different possibility and way of functioning. Depressions seemed to disappear for a while. It wasn't all of what I was looking for and I knew it was part of it. Reiki was the beginning of being aware that there were different possibilities and wow, maybe if I let go of a tiny bit of form, structure, control and rigidity, life might be just a little bit more fun and enjoyable!

I was married and my son who is now 18, was four then. I went on a mission to find some way to help my son, who had been labeled at age two with ADD and ADHD, and to ease his

discomfort. I had opted for no medications so I delved into everything I could find with Doreen Virtue, Sonja Choquette, and Wayne Dyer. I would guide my son through meditations every night and it seemed to help. For a bit. Putting him on a strict diet of no dyes and artificial flavorings and NEVER microwaving his food helped a bit also, until he would go to someone else's house. This was stressful and not fun.

A few years after starting Reiki and realizing that I required more, I got a phone call from a privately owned massage school. Yep! You guessed it! Off to massage school I went. I thought if I can "fix" bodies, I can just eliminate emotional junk people are trying to get rid of and can't seem to. What I learned was to turn on and tune into my awareness with people's bodies. Wow! This was another awareness of Hmm, maybe I'm not crazy, and maybe I am just aware.

I would find great joy when people would get off my table and their whole being was changed. They didn't hurt, they were relaxed and happy, for a short period of time. I knew I wanted to create lasting differences in people. I wanted to create big changes with people. I knew it was possible and that I didn't yet have all the tools I required.

Several years later I got a phone call from a rep at Integrative Institute for Nutrition out of New York. I had been researching David Wolfe and his Raw Food plans and somehow had clicked on being interested in health coaching. Yep! You guessed it again! Off to being a Health and Lifestyle Coach I went! By this time I had two more boys, one of which had severe allergies, asthma and some other things more behavior-related. All of his food had to be homemade, we couldn't go to certain people's houses because the animals gave him hives and so on. Once again I had created another situation of stress and no fun!

The Energy of Play

About five months into the Health program I was introduced to Access Consciousness. I went to my first Bars class and my life changed. I didn't know how it had changed or what had changed. I just knew that things were different. Something and shifted and nothing was the same as before.

Over the course of the last few years I have taken many Access classes. So part of Access is asking questions and looking for an awareness. There are also body processes, such as The Bars. Now my awareness had been opened wide up. Actually I was choosing to acknowledge my awareness, and with having questions to ask I was beginning to step out of judgment of myself and others and get rid of the vicious circles of stress and no fun I had created as my life. There are still ups and downs and discomfort and things like that. However, I now have the tools and the curiosity to choose something different.

So what the heck does all this have to do with playing and enjoying life? Do you remember the person forcing themselves to jog through the park and their body hurt and it just didn't seem to have any ease and flow to it at all? The one that was choosing pain and suffering? How many questions do you perceive that person asked their body before they decided to go for a jog? This is where using questions begins to get super fun. If we look into that person's universe with curiosity and wonderment, we may find something like programming and points of view this person had bought from somewhere.

Like we sit on the couch and think we are going to relax for a bit before we go to bed at night, and what shows up in the commercials? People with beautiful thin bodies. Say we choose instead to look at a magazine. Most people in magazines are thin and beautiful. We aren't asking questions like I wonder if this is Photoshopped or if my body would even like to look like that or is all this judgment I'm perceiving really even mine? We

are buying into this thing of "this is what people should look like, this is what people should do to get there" and everything lumped and glumped within all of that.

By not asking questions this person is going into judgment and conclusion that something is wrong and that the only way to "fix" it is to destroy their body with a predetermined regimen of diet and exercise. When you look into that person's universe, how much fun do you perceive? How much do you perceive this person playing? How much do you perceive that this person is limiting themselves?

So now check out the person who was flying through the park and their body was like Yes!!! This person wasn't exercising because they bought that they had to do this to create X result. They were doing this from the pure joy and fun of it.

Where do you find yourself functioning more often than not? Are you going through life with bricks for feet? Are you instead the energy of play and choosing for the fun of whatever?

I invite you to come play with me for a bit here and maybe have a smidgen of a glimpse of what could possibly change for you. Pick an area of your life that you think you have a "problem" with. I will give you a couple of different ways to play with this.

One of my favorite things about Access is that it's about empowering you to know what you know. Sometimes people will get frustrated with me because they are asking me questions looking for conclusions and answers, I instead I ask them questions! You see questions open the doors for possibilities and awareness, which lead to more choices, more possibilities and more awareness's. Conclusions and answers shut the doors of possibility and create a no-choice universe.

The Energy of Play

For me it's way more fun to play with questions and follow the energy.

Doesn't that sound more fun anyways? So let's pick a "problem" and see how we can play with that. Let's play with bodies for a bit. How is your body? Do you wake up in the morning happy and super excited to have the adventure of a new day? That's ok, I didn't used to either. How can we shift that for you? Surprise! You can start before you even get out of bed and ask a question! Something simple like "Who does this belong to?" would be a good start.

You see we are infinite beings that chose bodies in this lifetime because we are brilliant and smart! However, our body is the one thing we judge the most. It's the one thing we abuse the most and it's the one thing we love to ignore the most. We are absolutely brilliant and cutting off our awareness when it comes to our bodies. Isn't that awesome! We get up every morning and take for granted that our body is still with us, it carries us through the day, it wears the fabulous clothes we buy, and it drives our cars, and so on. We have been taught to exclude the one thing that is always there for us, EVERY day of our lives!

How often do you go through the day totally fine and then BAM! You are instantly grumpy, or wow, all of the sudden you have a headache, or you go into a store and dang it, your feet hurt, what's wrong with your shoes? Your feet didn't hurt before you got to the store! There is a very simple solution for this. 98 percent of the thoughts that go through your head, the feelings that you perceive in your body (like pain), and the emotions you swear are absolutely yours, none of that belongs to you. Isn't that exciting? I'll say it again. 98 percent of the thoughts, feelings and emotions that you perceive are not yours.

Ha!! I can hear you. I didn't believe it at first either. I thought

only psychic people could do that and I certainly didn't think I was psychic. I had just taken a four-day Foundation and Level 1 Access Consciousness class and I went to pick my son up from a friend's house. The instant he got in the car my head hurt. I actually asked a question: "Who does this belong to?"

I looked at him and asked "Do you have a headache?" He says, "YES! For two days now!" I thought wow, that's cool, and did the return to sender and "my" headache was gone.

I have seen this work with my clients and my children. It's like a magic wand of sorts. This isn't just for headaches, this can be for everything. Remember? Thoughts, feelings and emotions. That basically covers everywhere that you currently function!

Here's a fun activity to play with. This is a three-day assignment. We play with this in Access all the time. For every thought, feeling and emotion that comes up in your universe ask "Who does this belong to?" Here's the key. Ask from the space of curiosity and wonderment. Not from the space of expectation and conclusion. Ok? It's about the energy you be when you ask a question that creates the change. A statement and a conclusion can have a question mark at the end also. A true question is something you don't have an answer for.

The next thing you can ask is "Is it mine, somebody else's or something else's?" The truth makes you feel lighter and a lie makes you feel heavier. So what's true for you will be expansive and more spacious. What's not true for you will feel heavy and dense. So what if it's not yours? Return it to sender with consciousness attached. Then the clearing statement (www.TheClearingStatement.com).

If you do this for three days from the space of curiosity, you will feel like you are in a walking talking meditation. That in

itself will change a mega ton of things in your body. What if there is not actually anything wrong with you or your body? What if you are just having tons of awareness's?

Now I will share with you my magic wand. In Access we have this phrase called the clearing statement. This is a bunch of short speak for clearing things from anywhere and everywhere that we could possibly clear things. From any lifetime, any dimension, any realm, anywhere in the present and also for the future. This covers the polarities that we have bought into: everything that's right and everything that's wrong, everything that's good, everything that's bad and so on.

When I first was introduced to this I refused to say it out loud, someone might think I really was crazy! However as crazy as it sounded it worked. Here's my favorite part with this. I learned energy work in a very old school sort of fashion. Where you ponder on something and analyze it and pick it apart and so on and so forth. I'm a little ADD and half the time it took so long to do all that and try to meditate on it that I forgot what the heck I was doing! If I did remember, nothing really seemed to change. So when I started to play with the clearing statement boy was I excited when things started to change, and super quick! Basically this is how it works.

When you have an energetic charge on something it sticks it in your automatic response system somewhere in your universe. So say for example that you have children and they know all the buttons to push to light you up. Seems like my youngest, who is 5 right now, has a radar for finding toys in any store we go to. Do you see where I'm going with this? Yep! You've already got the visual movie playing in your head! Typical scenario where everyone in the store knows that I said "No, we are not buying that toy today." He's super dramatic about it, super loud and great at drawing attention. My auto response used to be "just

give him what he wants so he will stop", "everyone's looking at me be quiet." However, now I have this magic wand called the clearing statement and I also have tools now, like asking questions.

Get guys that things sometimes do take time to change depending on your points of view, and know that creating change also has a starting point. I realized that my reaction to him throwing fits in the store triggered responses in me that I had taken on as a child. I grew up in a pretty strict home and temper tantrums were absolutely never allowed. Having a point of view was considered being sassy and rude.

How many times as a child did you vow that you would never be like your parents, then you grow up and have kids of your own and then one day they do something and you realize you are repeating the same patterns that your parents did with you? Or you realize that you were in such resistance to the way you were raised that you go totally opposite in the other direction. Kind of like I have done with my youngest.

So when you have those awarenesses now you can ask a question. "Who does that belong to?" You may have a super clear awareness or it may just be that the energy shifts and changes when you ask. Then you say the rest: Return to sender with consciousness attached and then the clearing statement.

Isn't that fun? I'm in the store, my son is being loud and expressing himself, I was able to ask a question, I had all these awareness's as a result of asking a question, I cleared it, the energy shifted. He might still be being loud and drawing attention, but the significance and the energetic charge this originally had totally vanished. Now this was all done from the space of curiosity. I used to not be able to get out of the frustration of that and I would allow situations like that to

The Energy of Play

totally ruin the rest of my day. It's so much more fun for me to function in the space of creativity, fun and play that when I am aware that I'm going the other direction I now choose to change it.

Have you ever heard the saying "Happiness is a choice"? That actually used to tick me off when I would hear that. Which is actually pretty funny. I have been told all my life things like "You are too happy, nobody should ever be that happy in the mornings, you laugh too much, why is everything so funny to you, don't you ever get mad." I didn't have the tools prior to Access and it certainly didn't occur to me to ask a question. Have you ever tried to pretend you are grumpy when that really isn't your reality? It's interesting, I'm not suggesting that you try it. Your body does all kinds of strange things like gain a bunch of weight without having to eat extra food to accomplish that, hormones go out of balance, your hair falls out by the handfuls and getting out of bed in the morning is a major chore.

Here's the thing with the clearing statement and the simple little question of "Who does this belong to?" When you ask a question, going into the logic of the awareness and all the details of it is not required. Picking it apart, pondering over all the aspects of it, which for me I would go into more wrongness of myself and judgment that I had even created the issue in the first place, and in so doing I was actually sticking the thing I was looking to change and clear, deeper and deeper into my universe and reality. So the clearing statement does all the work for you.

Do you see how much less effort, time and energy that takes? When you clear the energetic charge of something that's sticking you, it's like the "thing" disappears. It doesn't matter where it came from, where or who you bought it from and decided it was your "thing," it doesn't matter what it is or how

long you have had it as your "thing." It is all choice. If you are truly looking to change your life, to create more joy, fun and laughter, to have a life of ease, it truly is just a choice.

Let's play with another fun tool. In Access we have these things called the 10 keys, or the 10 commandments. One of them is No Judgment. Now growing up in a religious home, my first thought was "what the heck is No Judgment doing in my reality again?" In the bible it says "Thou shalt not judge." I loved the idea of No Judgment and in the same space I was in resistance to it, Big Time. I had watched people stand up in church and give speeches on not judging and then turn around and judge the heck out of everything and everyone. Being the recipient of a lot of judgment throughout my life I was curious to see how this would be different taught through Access.

Here are a few key points I have learned with judgment through Access. Judgment is the most toxic thing we put in our bodies. Isn't that funny? Not food, judgment. Don't believe me? I invite you to play with it, just for fun! When you get up in the morning and you look in the mirror, what are your first thoughts? I'm guessing it's not "Good morning beautiful!" or "Thank you for being here with me another day!" or "Wow, I'm so excited to have this body, I wonder what fun we could have today!" I'm guessing it's more like, "My butt is so big, that's gross" or "Dang saggy boobs" or "really, more wrinkles." Do you see how much easier it has become for us to wake up and start our day with the litany of judgment? It's just that our body is usually the first thing we look at every day. It's also the thing we judge the most.

There have been scientific studies done where the scientists have played with projecting thoughts, feelings and emotions at molecules and things like water crystals. What they have found is that everything starts with a thought feeling or an emotion, like disease. So disease is just dis-ease in the body. For example,

The Energy of Play

take something like depression. With manic depression, people weren't born with that, and they didn't just "wake up" one morning with it. If you walk them back through their lives, most of the time, their parents were like that to a certain extent, or their friends were like that. You see things we pick up things from everyone and everywhere. Especially as children we are like sponges. This is the way Dad or Mom is, these are their points of views, this is what they look like, and this is the way they talk and so on.

The really cool thing is their life doesn't have to be your life. You can actually choose to be you. It's ok! So if you look at depression, it's becoming one of the biggest epidemics in health issues. If you listen to a "depressed" person talk, do you perceive their body and being just oozing with judgment? It's like you go away wanting to take a shower and wash all that off! So check this out. Your fat cells are where you hold your toxins in your body. So if you are feeding your body a plethora of judgment, what does your body look like? What does your body feel like? What is the energy level in your body? So everything that brings up and let's down would you like to destroy and uncreate all that? The clearing statement works with anything and everything so you can play with it anywhere and everywhere!

In Access we say "Your point of view creates your reality". So if your point of view is that you shall judge the heck out of yourself and everything else, what have you created as your reality? What have you created with your body?

For every judgment you hold in place, it doesn't matter what it is on or about, for every judgment there are 25 other ones holding that one in place. For each of the 25 there are 1 holding those in place and it keeps on going. It's like the ultimate multi-level marketing company that you hold in place as the

structure that you call your life and reality. Do you see how exhausting that is? Do you see how much energy it takes to keep all that in place? No wonder you aren't having fun! No wonder depression is running rampid!

So what are some steps to changing that? Every time you find yourself going into judgment, here is a clearing for you:

"Everywhere I have aligned and agreed and resisted and reacted to… (whatever it is) I destroy and uncreate it." (Go to www.TheClearingStatement.com for the complete clearing statement.)

You can also ask "Who does this belong to?" Remember you are super aware and 98% of the thoughts, feelings and emotions that you perceive are not yours? So I wonder how many judgments are you picking up on, sticking in your body, and limiting yourself with that aren't even yours? Interesting awareness, right?

The other thing with judgments I would like to share with you is this. If everything is made up of cells and molecules, and projected thoughts, feelings and emotions impact and change the structure of cells and molecules, and judgment is the biggest toxin we feed our body, what is your awareness of what judgment does to the planet? To the plants and animals? To every creature seen and unseen? It's killing the planet. Somehow that doesn't seem very playful and fun to me.

A reality is something that two or more people align and agree upon. So if you want to create a change, I wonder would you be willing to start with yourself? Depression, cancer, diabetes, I could go on and on. Those aren't the epidemics. Those are the effects of judgment. So you could say we have an epidemic of judgment.

The Energy of Play

When I go to Access classes and come home it's like Christmas. At class we clear all kinds of things that come up and create all this change within ourselves. The magical part is when you don't hold in place and make significant your judgments and points of view, it allows the space for those around you to change as well. Most of this change is not cognitive. I had heard people talk about this, and once again I was like "there's no way that's possible". Until I came home from my first class that I had been gone for four days for. My little guys made a mess on the floor and before I could do or say anything, my husband grabbed the vacuum and cleaned up the mess. I have been with him for 19 years and that was the first time he had ever used the vacuum. I'm here to tell you, changing your points of views can change your reality and those around you. It's like magic with zero effort!

If you are looking to change your body, your life, your living, and your reality I wonder if you would be willing to play with some of these tools and questions. I wonder, what questions could you ask to unsnuff your playfulness? I wonder if you aren't carrying around and sticking all that stuff that you have picked up from other people into your body, would your life be more fun? Could you find a moment each day to ask "body, what would be fun for you today?"

Can you perceive that even letting go of a teeny tiny bit of something can create phenomenal changes? Can you perceive the way your body has lightened up just a bit, just by having an awareness and asking the few simple questions? So I wonder, are you ready to play? Are you ready to step out of your box and be you? I wonder who else in your life is asking for this, and what contribution could you be there?

Thank you for playing with me. If you would like some more information on the clearing statement you can visit:

www.TheClearingStatement.com. If you are interested in playing with me more in the future you can find all of my info and how to reach me in the bio! Thank you so much for the contribution you be.

About the Author

Janie Lin Smith

Janie Lin Smith is the CEO of Conscious Creations and is known as The Energetic Health Coach, #1 Bestselling Author in the book "I'm Having It," a former Access Consciousness® Certified Facilitator, Certified Massage Therapist, Health Coach, Entrepreneur, Reiki Master, Energy healer, Speaker, Tester of multi-level marketing companies (29 different times with 29 different companies), Mother of three boys (18, 7 and 5), World Traveler, Creator of ease, space and magic in people's lives, Editor, Phenomenal facilitator of inspiring people to step into their potency and create beyond what they could only have imagined in the past. Creator of Fabulous At 40.

Janie Lin is the embodiment of "Having It", Change, Growth, Laughter, Fun, and stepping outside of comfort zones. From being the "lone Ranger" in bringing a practice of Access Consciousness® to a town where not many were super interested in changing, growing and expanding, to traveling the world to

attend Access classes (Costa Rica, Mexico, Australia, London, Florida), to continuing to expand her life and living even in the face of ridicule and judgment.

"Staying put" is not her forte, Janie Lin grew up in a family of travelers. Her playground was the Oregon coast, Southern California coast, New Mexico, Alaska, Idaho, Nevada, the western slope of Colorado, and currently the Arizona desert in Phoenix. By the time she graduated high-school she had been to 17 different schools. With the ocean as her heart song and the mountains as inspiration she continues to create beyond without limitations.

Janie Lin is zany, spontaneous and fun. Often she is told she's too happy, or she's having too much fun. Her husband has long since quit telling her she can't be, do or have something. A few years ago he "decided" Janie Lin needed a "job". He "brought her home "a stone and landscape supply business. After a couple of years spent playing in that Janie Lin chose to sell it. Everyone in the circle of family and friends told her it couldn't be done. It would never sell. It wasn't worth anything. Utilizing the tools of Access Consciousness® and choosing to attend a yearlong course with two Access Facilitators, Janie Lin doubled her selling price and sold the business. Time frame using the tools of Access: three months. As you can imagine it was a shock to the "circle"!

Janie Lin is the creator of 9 Elements to Awaken and include You in Your Life, Speaking the Universal Language ~ Talking to the Elementals, C.H.O.I.C.E. To Have It All, and other classes where she incorporates the tools of Access Consciousness. 9 Elements is a program where Janie Lin facilitates you in creating a Deal and Deliver with yourself, which creates you showing up as you in your life. Talking to the Elementals is a program where Janie Lin combines the phenomenal energetic capacities

the earth has to gift with the potency and magic of bodies. Her greatest joy comes from creating the space for people choose their greatness and step into their magic and potency. Whether it's her children, people in her classes, her clients, or people she meets in everyday life. Her inspiration and targets are to create awareness in people to know what's true for them, and to be a contribution to expanding consciousness, the planet and everything included in that.

A sought-after facilitator, Janie Lin also offers tele-seminars, Google Hangouts, webinars, and workshops worldwide. Janie Lin also facilitates some of the classes of Access Consciousness®:

- The Bars
- 10 Keys
- The How To Become Money Workbook Class (C.H.O.I.C.E. To Have It All: Roadmap to create -your Money Magick)
- Fabulous At 40 – Empowering women to live their best life now!
- And much more!

To schedule a workshop in your area and to reach out to her go to:

www.janielinsmith.com
janiehealthcoach@gmail.com
Facebook: https://www.facebook.com/consciouscreations14
Twitter: https://twitter.com/janielin147
Amazon Author Page: https://www.amazon.com/author/janiesmith

CHAPTER

10

Don't Make Me Grow Up!

Lisa Miller

It was always a foggy or frosty morning when the farmer across the road beeped on his old Landrover horn, signalling he was ready to feed out the hay to the cows. My younger brother and I would sprint out the door, already dressed and excited by the thought of Mr. Jew coming on his usual Saturday hay feeding session. The cow's breath would be like trumpets of steam as they also waited in growing excitement. Of course they didn't really show it like we did but meandered over to the fence and headed down to where they were usually feed. With a troupe of neighbourhood children on the back of his trailer Mr. Jew would purposely drive through the pot holes and puddles knowing we might get wet or have to scramble to hold on to the bouncing hay bales. I would nearly be in tears if I missed his beep of the horn or we were not at home when he arrived. Cutting the bales and pushing the hay off the back is one of my favourite childhood memories. The cows would meander behind the trailer then stop with heads lowered and

ignore the action around them. It was always really exciting when he let us drive his Landrover down the gulley and through the shallow streams that formed in a Waikato winter. No one even knew exactly what time he would show up and whose turn it was on trailer or in the cab and no one really minded as we were following a natural instinct to just play along and follow fun till it shifted to another time or space. On stary nights we would climb the tallest hill on his farm and look up to the stars imagining other worlds, UFOS and strange being. During the muggy summer heat we would climb that same hill and push down homemade go carts that could only stop by hitting a fence or stump at the bottom. Often I would go home with grass stains on my levis jeans, prickles in my hands and mud on my face.

The old house that had burnt to the ground, leaving only a crumbling brick chimney and pot belly oven became my own home - mud pies were baked in the stove, babies were rocked and put to bed in the long grass and crumbling foundations, friends were entertained and were poured endless cups of imaginary tea. Clay banks near the house were the ingredients in our mud pies and also made the implements we cooked in. I was so disappointed when they cleared that site and it sat as an empty section with runaway wild flowers and grass for years. To me this encapsulates the energy of playfulness - the total abandonment to be present to what is around you and following our natural inclination to play.

The energy of play is the hint of a new day and the energy of expectation. Playfulness for me is all about following the energy and not knowing which direction and what you will find. For me following the energy of playfulness is the easiest way for me to create my life. I know that when I follow the light expansive feelings I will find fun and play somewhere on the way. Not knowing how, when, where is the exciting part and

The Energy of Play

when it shows up it's even more expansive as you are totally in the moment and not judging how it came to be or where it's leading.

The energy of play. What is it for me? It's the whisper of excitement and freedom that starts somewhere in my body. It's the possibility of connecting with the infinite being that is truly me. It's the beginning of something new created in the world like the shoot of a newly grown tree set amongst a backdrop of mature trees. It's the promise of connecting with other playful beings. As a child my work or job was to play and have fun as it is for most children. As children we see it as our job and we know it is as natural as a mother suckling her young. That's how it was for me and still is. It is one of my greatest gifts – the propensity for play and finding fun in even the most seemingly dire situations. The one who is giggling at a friend's funeral because I have remembered funny times together; told off in meetings for laughing too much at the end of a long day, known far and wide as having a quirky sense of humour and for being loud! I have been on my own with my two children the past two years and it was a choice I made as I was no longer having fun in my marriage and it felt like I was dying a little more each day. The energy of play was hard for me to connect with and my choice was for myself to reconnect with that energy so my family could function from that energy and have more fun.

I grew up in a small, rural, working class town in New Zealand. From a young age I recognised the energy of play and knew that if I followed it I would learn so much and it would expand my life. Small children recognise this and play is their work and in playing they are learning and practising how to be on this planet. As we get older this energy of playfulness can be suppressed due to schooling, parents and other people's expectations and judgments. At times this was so for me too however I always perceived that recognising opportunities for

play and allowing others to play was my gift and not something everybody could do, I became a teacher and then got paid to bring the energy of play back into learning.

If we copied children and followed this energy of play we could create happier, more fulfilling and richer experiences at the drop of hat. When this energy is allowed out of the box it opens us up to anything is possible and in being in the moment all so called stresses are gone. It is extremely hard to be angry, sad or any other heavy, contracting energy when you are laughing and playing.

Why do adults stop this energy from expanding? JUDGMENTS. We are so wired in this reality to judge everything that even our so called positive judgments are limiting. If we say something is good then it can only be good and when it isn't good then we are left wanting. Marriages and families often full prey to this - we judge that our parents are good at something so then it stops them from being even better than good. When they stop being good we are left with disappointment and other heavy, contracting energies.

Instead of judgments if we operate out of asking questions which lifts us into a lighter more expansive energy then having fun, playing and creating are possible. Authentic playfulness is not something that is planned for, you can anticipate it could be playful and we often perceive something will be fun and playful when we get that feelings of excitement in our tummies. Often this feeling is misidentified as fear. Our expectations and projections can stop the energy showing up too. Have you noticed when you have an expectation of having fun and you have already judged how it will pan out it often doesn't, our projections are full of judgments and stop the energy of play just developing naturally? When it doesn't show up as we thought it would then we judge it even more

The Energy of Play

and the energy of play disappears and a contrived inauthentic situation occurs instead.

In my experience playfulness actually connects us to our creative self too. How many things have been created in the world when people have just been playing around – experimenting, having fun and following that light, joyful energy. I have chosen to do this in the past two years and my life is expanding as a result. When I sense that playful energy I follow it and I don't question where it's taking me I just go and it's leading me to more play which results in more happiness and something wonderful being created that surprises me daily. More happiness equates to more play which leads to more happiness and so on.

So how do you know if you are not following that energy? I used to hear people say they were following the energy and to me is was just semantics. I had no sense what the energy was and how to find it. Luckily I found people in my life who could mentor me and I am currently developing the energy muscle. First thing to do is to be authentic about where you are at. Go beyond what you think other people would say or think about you and write down how it is for you. If you aren't having enough fun and play and creating an amazing life then you aren't following energy but living in this causal reality which pulls us into a cause and effect universe where we are at the effect of circumstances, other people's judgments and expectations of us. Ask yourself: Am I having fun? Is this something that will continue to be fun for me? Will I be able to be playful in this job/house/relationship/friendship/business?

To really notice this energy you will need to drop your barriers and attempt to expand your own being out as far as you can. Sit quickly and imagine you as an energetic being growing and growing until you take up the whole planet. Now

try to expand poverty and make it bigger. It will disappear or be a heavy contracted feeling. That is because there isn't really poverty in this world - there is enough abundance for everyone. Now think about your gratitude for your child or a loved one - now imagine this yummy energy expanding out of your body. It will feel light and airy and expandable. This is the energy that we need to follow. You will need to practice this like any sport you learn or new skill. Imagine events or people in your life and see if you can expand the energy of that event/person outside of you. If you have a social event you have been invited to imagine the energy of it growing. If it doesn't feel light and expansive then don't go to it if you don't have to!!

I know this can take time - don't worry it has taken me over 40 years to start to really do this and real friends and family won't judge you for not doing something.

Another thing you can do is to allow time to just BE in your hectic schedule. Turn off the internet, TV, sit up after the children go to bed, stay home instead of going shopping and give yourself half an hour of you time. In this time you could meditate, read a book, draw a picture, write, have a long bath, bask in the sunshine, sit in dim lights with candles burning - whatever it takes to unwind. I have found with experience removing myself for a short period of time daily or as much as I can in a busy week allows me to connect back to me. Not the Mum, Sister, daughter, lover, friend, employee me but the real me that was is always there under these other shadows of our existence. All the expectations and projections of who we have to be in these various roles actually stop us from reconnecting with our playful selves. In this reality we are taught that if we have something then we can do something, then finally we can be something. For example, getting my teaching degree was having a degree, doing a job so I could be a great teacher. What I have learnt in the past five years through some challenging

The Energy of Play

yet expansive experiences the true flow of life is the opposite way - BE, DO, HAVE. We are human beings not human doings and I have experienced through using tools that support and encourage me to be the real me I get into action and I end up having what I desire. Obviously there is some action needed and there are plenty of opportunities for me to expand the energy of play in my life. As I said before so much is created out of this spontaneous energy. This is the being part that is often missed out of our lives as we go about just doing stuff which we hope gives us stuff.

What is it you know about the energy of play? This is my take on it and I know you will have your own interesting take on it too. Ask yourself every morning What do I know about the energy of play? What more can I add to my life to create more playfulness? It may seem risky for some of you as you haven't really played in a very long time and you were told that it is childish or you're too old for that behaviour. I say BE CHILDISH. How many children do you know going grey, staying home to finish something, missing out on meals or good times because they are too busy, having major health issues because they are put no focus on exercise? I am not aspiring to grow up but grow in - grow back into my true playful self that was there the moment I was born, grow into that comfortable place in me that feels like home, grow into a light, expansive being that is fun to be around, grow into my own space of joy and possibility. Anything is possible when you play in your energy of play.

About the Author

Lisa Miller

Lisa Miller was born in New Zealand in 1969 to parents who knew how to have fun. If she wasn't playing outside on the farm across the road she was reading a book and read voraciously. Lisa wanted to be a teacher from a young age and at the age of 23 she finished her degree and taught Primary School in New Zealand before heading to London for four years. Travelling became a huge passion and still is. She is a facilitator in a business called Lift above limitations, has two children, and now lives in a sleepy seaside town in the North Island of New Zealand. She still reads but also learnt to surf at 40 and spends all year round in the water. In the past four years a change in circumstances and numerous losses in her life has led her to now support women and families through grief, loss and change. The tools she has learnt in the past few years has led her to transcending problems and creating a happier life. Writing has always been a way for Lisa to process things and she still has letters she wrote to her grandparents at five and letters she wrote to her family when she was living in London in the 90s.

www.accesslisamiller.com
accesslisamiller@gmail.com
Facebook page : lift above limitations, Whakatane New Zealand

CHAPTER

11

Playing with Everything!

Christel Crawford

I was invited.

"The Energy of Play," she said.

It was light, but there was also this.... Meh. Ugh.

"Oh, cool!" I said.

I couldn't get the resistance out of my world about it. And it was hangin' me up!

"What do I know about play?!"

Play..... play..... argh.... play?! Really?

And I'm sitting here writing about something I thought I knew nothing about because it's been friggin' light, despite all my

resistance, and I've got big elephant tears streaming down my face.

Because as I'm writing about something "I don't know anything about," I'm seeing how much I've always known. Trusted. Really, I've spent most of my life looking at my past and just chuckling at how crazy it was. At how crazy I was. Shaking my head and face-palming.

But today, I'm seeing something different. I'm seeing… what was right about me that I just wasn't getting. I'm seeing how willing I was just to…play. Even when I was judging myself, there was something that I knew.

Today, I'm playing with the Universe very differently….and I'm learning new things all the time. Today it's a bit more like a whisper, rather than a shout. There is more finesse, and awareness, and kindness.

And it's that capacity I've had that is still creating me in ways I'm only now beginning to see and claim.

And this morning, I'm writing all of this sitting outside. The morning air is cool. The air inside the house is hot. The day is full of things I could do. Should do. From anyone else's point of view, I have things I should be worried about, frantically creating. But something has changed for me.

Consciousness has become a bit of a buzz word lately. And I can fairly say that I've been creating a conscious life for almost two years now.

One of the things we Access Consciousness® folk talk about is following the energy.

The Energy of Play

Following the energy is one of the most airy-fairy things I've ever done. It has connotations of smoking a lot of weed, long flowered skirts and irresponsibility. It doesn't fit in to any paradigm that anyone has any respect for. But this demand in my universe for consciousness, awareness, has created this airy-fairy path of awesomeness.

The thing is, we live in a totally magnanimous universe – a universe that is looking to give us what we're asking for! So, when we ask, "How can this day get any worse?"

The universe goes, "Ok! That's what you want – I'll show you!"

But when we dare to ask: How does it get any better than this? The Universe shows us. I'll show you how it gets better… there's this… and this… and then we keep asking, how does it get better? And it just keeps getting better.

So, with questions, and following your awareness of the energy, of asking a question and then following what's light for you, you end up receiving gifts from the Universe that go beyond anything you could have dreamed up yourself. It turns out that following the energy is a whole big pile'a play.

When I first started Access Cosnciousness, I heard the word 'play' all the time. People use it even when their face doesn't know they're doing it, and you look at them cock-eyed and ask "Really??"

Joy. Play. Lightness.

{eye roll} Jesus - shut up already.

I had spent so many years just trying to get to happy. For me Access® was the next step in that 'trying'. At the start of my

Access® journey, I was still slogging it out in the mud-fields of reckless emotions and what felt like an interminable ocean of 'stuff' that didn't even have a remote third cousin related to lightness, play and joy.

All this positivity BS just needed to go.

And then this kicker: my middle name is Joy.

My mom always tells me stories about my name. Or 'the' story about my name. How when she first saw me, when they first put me in her arms, she cried and thought I was the most beautiful thing she'd ever seen. And she wanted to name me the most beautiful name she could think of: Christel Joy. She thought it sounded like angels and tinkling bells and wonder.

"How many times do I have to hear that," I would say through clenched teeth in my mind, resistance going off like popcorn.

Can anyone else FEEL the eye-rolling taking place here?

Her voice always lightens about four notches above normal when she's telling it and she gets a smile in it, like she's still looking lovingly down at my new baby body every time.

And she always chooses to tell it -right- before she tells me that I'll always be her baby girl and then somehow squeezes in the request for more money.

Arrrrrrrrrghhhhhhhhhhh.

And here's the final annoying thing: my childhood was anything BUT joy. There were no angels. Or tinkling bells. My childhood was a dimly lit cave where sharp objects fell from the ceiling at random times and usually on your head.

The Energy of Play

I blocked out most of it, but of the stuff I can remember, I was scared most of the time, terrified the rest of it: unsure, shy and lonely. Not exactly the descriptors of "It's a Wonderful Life". And my mother, as nice as she'll be to you when you first meet her, is literally one of the most manipulative and controlling people I've ever met. Think Stepford Wives, low-income version.

So of course, at some point I decided that playing was for weak and stupid people, and I was not the playin' kind. The oldest of five and the watcher in a very tumultuous family, I always stayed to the side. I was babysitting, watching, waiting for that one kid to be too loud so I could shush them, that other kid to pick a fight so I could stop them, that mom to get triggered by some other kid so that I could intervene. Our life was a shitstorm of potential conflict and I seemed to be the only one who cared to change it. I remember consciously staying out of the 'fray' of play so that I could watch and keep everyone safe from everyone else. Any kid who chose to try to get me to play would get a "look" and a fierce, "Don't" to which there was no questioning.

My understanding of play always happened when I was by myself, and usually involved some imaginary trip down a novel's lane, or a movie… and later on, there was definitely that vibrator behind my bed…and even later, dancing and boys. So, to say that I brought strength, will, work ethic and fierce demand into my adult world is to grossly understate. I was a fierce warrior for staying alive who only played at the "appropriate" times and got annoyed when people played out of turn. However, because of my family, I became a master at surviving. My family ran on a paradigm of never-enough. Each child support payment was allocated before it ever arrived, and overspent when it did. But even when I was going through the phase of daring to have my own opinion and

getting kicked out of the house about every three days, I always had a roof over my head. There was the eight days in jail, and the five different friends I stayed with between jail and losing my job, and the few days I slept in my car; but I was never homeless. And somehow, I managed to create new tires for my car when I didn't have the money, and generated people giving me $5000 to go to China and I smuggled Bibles and stuff...

There was something I knew about play.

Why do I say that? I mean, really... why do I follow up a survival conversation with a statement as bold as "There was something I knew about play"?

Are those related?

Well when you look at the energy of play, there is a lot of lightness in it. There is a lot of kindness. There is a lot of just losing yourself in the process and an innate trust that you'll not only be okay but that everything will be magnificent and wonder-filled. And of course there will be dinner at the end of the day and a warm set of arms to hold you.

So, in the middle of the chaotic electric-storm that was my life, there was still a knowing that no matter what, I would be okay. And the more I got into the world, the more I saw the effect of my choices on people and what that created for me. The more playful I was when I was waiting tables, the more money I made. The more people wanted to come sit in my section. The more playful I was at the club, the more I got asked to dance. The more dates I went on. The more playful I was on dates, the more they wanted to just give me. The more playful I was...the more. And the more. And the more. The more ease that was created. The more joy. The more people feeling comfortable. The more.

The Energy of Play

I mean, most children play. With everything.

The dirt pile in the back yard is an ocean housing a massive castle on a island with a large moat. Dragons fly there without permits and massive amounts of hose water spell disaster and glee.

The dandelions in the yard are the bouquets we get married with, the wreathes that circle our head, and the gifts we know will brighten Mommy's day. The chalk on the sidewalk creates the masterpieces that should be saved, the hopscotch lines that we can't fall outside of and the message of love to Daddy for when he gets home.

As kids, we GET what it takes to create life the way we would like it, and we don't think about it. We just Be it.

I never knew that I be'd it. I was so busy focusing on all the un-magic that I failed to notice the magic.

In fact it took a pretty dramatic afternoon for me to hit the bottom of my point of view and start coming up again.

It was one hot August day. Birds chirping, flowers blooming, and with everyone else inside taking a much-deserved sweet afternoon nap, I was collapsed on the side lawn, sobs drilling my heart and body into the ground, not sure if I was ever going to be able to peel myself off the grass ever again. I was totally done being on the planet, and completely chicken sh*t to do anything potentially damaging and un-fatal. And so a good hour of sobbing later, I'd decided that a sufficient amount of booze would cause a blackout, and all the former done in a bathtub, would cause my body to gently sink under, creating an easy, permanent, nice-and-fatal end.

Seriously, I just couldn't get my life to work for me. It didn't seem to matter what I did.

What book I read. What church I went to. Everything I knew up to that point to get my world to work, wasn't working. I was sad all the time. I was offended for the rest of it.

Lonely to a point of wanting to crawl away forever.

And then as I really got into it, something in my head just went: Hey. Hey. Stop. Stop. What are we doing here… my love… my Christel…What are we doing? And something changed. Something just shifted in me. I knew, at that moment, something had to change. It wasn't me offing myself in a residential amount of water. It was something else. Something that just HAD to be able to change this for me. Change SOMETHING. Anything.

And a week later, a friend I'd just met, referred me a practitioner not far from me who started helping me get back on my feet again. And a year and a half later, I found Access Consciousness.

If you've never taken any Access classes and this is making your baby hairs stand on end, please check it out. It's one of the most amazing sets of tools I've ever come across. Gary Douglas is the founder, Dain Heer is the co-creator. And Blossom Benedict has her own business and is a huge player as well. I recently took a class with Blossom, and she said something I'm sure she's said before, but was heard by me for the first time.

She said that there is likely an area of your life where you've always functioned from consciousness. From the energy of question. And wonder.

But listen: there's a lot of us really super aware folk on the planet

The Energy of Play

who cope with the ridiculous amounts of energetic information we pick up on in crazy ways. We get depressed. We drink. We drug. We have too much sex with too many people. A lot of us self-destruct in some way. So, that super-cool area where we function as magic usually gets lost in the melee of distraction, to the point where we can't see it - us - at all.

This was where I was at. Not being able to see that the area of most magic has always been this energy — of play.

We're never taught that we're energy.
Oh — did I mention that?
You are.
Energy.
Space.
Consciousness.
A beautiful bundle of conscious molecules just waiting for direction.
And everything you say - every thought you have - every point of view you take - creates you and your molecules' reality.
Weird, right?
So, in everyday life, we use a lot of words, but most of what gets created is created without words. It's created by the energy of it.

Have you ever noticed that when you're around a playful person you can't help but get drawn into their magical web? Have you ever thought to think that maybe the universe is drawn in in the same way? That by playing you're making yourself utterly irresistible?

And that's what I got that I was being without even knowing it. I was playing.

Energetically asking "What else is possible?" Energetically

tugging the Universe into my court, knowing that it would never let me fall. Playing with the molecules and not even knowing it.

Now that I know it, it's getting a little bit silly.

I've laughed more today than I have in I-can't-remember-when. The day started out with a totally blank canvas. Meaning, my mind. It was gone. These classes I take with Access Consciousness are unbelievably powerful, and today, post-class, I couldn't get a thought to come into or stay in my head. Sitting at my computer, freshly showered, I had "promised" each one of my online Facebook groups a post. Something wise regarding my teaser from the night before. About the energy of your life and living. And there was literally nothing. I couldn't think of anything to say, my brain was so blank from the weekend's class. I laughed again. Following Gary Douglas' advice to just show up and let the words fall out, I started writing and they did. I re-read them. Haha - brilliant.

While my beautiful friend was being her amazing self and making us both breakfast and I was searching for my mind, I got curious about what it would take to be paid as a public speaker. I Googled just that. A really great website popped up - a blog post by an irreverent diva out of who-knows-where that made me laugh and gave me food and fodder for the email I'd been wanting to send and create for my creation group. Her video made me laugh and gave me the inspiration I required to create in that moment what was asking to be created. And then "out of the blue", an email popped into my inbox literally an hour later - totally unrelated - titled: Wanna get paid to speak to people?

Woven in through the whole morning was this curiosity about my class, The Kindness of Sex. My friend messaged me over

Facebook, mid-digestion and pre-telecall wanting to talk about it, and in five minutes, we had a class created brand new in the UK and an email sent off for a conversation with one of his major contacts. Starting the tele-call for my creation group, I was still mind-blank, agenda-less. But I got on the call just totally curious about what it was going to be, about what was going to be created… and 49 minutes later, a fabulous tele-call had been birthed.

Irresistible Magic

So what if play was really about acknowledging the irresistible magic that you already be? When you look at your life, haven't you always gotten what you desired? I mean, really… if you wanted it, wasn't it yours? And so, is it possible, that you are more powerful than you've ever cared to notice? It turns out I was wrong about me… and I'm just wondering… if you are quite possibly wrong about you… and there is MUCH more right about you than you've ever acknowledged…
I'm betting on it.
XO.

About the Author

CHRISTEL CRAWFORD

Christel Crawford travels the world facilitating classes, coaching people and entrepreneurs worldwide. and creating a thriving business.

A magnificent creator, Christel empowers and invites her clients to create their lives and business with ease, joy and the creation of income based on the tools of Access Consciousness, their own brilliant awareness, and the success of the creation of her own life and business.

Published, writing and ever-creating, she lives in Vancouver, near the beach, and if she's not on or near her laptop, can be found on a massage table, a dance floor, or in a bookstore – exhaling deeply and laughing wildly about something.

THE END

About Happy Publishing

Happy Publishing is a full-service publishing house with an eclectic mix of books for your health, wealth and entertainment.

www.HappyPublishing.net for more information!

www.ingramcontent.com/pod-product-compliance
Lightning Source LLC
Chambersburg PA
CBHW071511150426
43191CB00009B/1482